Best Friends
with God

Also by Christy Bower:

Devotion Explosion: Getting Real with God

Best Friends
with God

*Falling in Love
with the God
Who Loves You*

Christy Bower

DISCOVERY HOUSE

PUBLISHERS®

Discovery House Publishers is affiliated with RBC Ministries,
Grand Rapids, Michigan.

Requests for permission to quote from this book should be directed to:
Permissions Department, Discovery House Publishers,
P.O. Box 3566, Grand Rapids, MI 49501 or contact us by e-mail at
permissionsdept@dhp.org

Scripture taken from the NEW AMERICAN STANDARD BIBLE®,
Copyright © 1960, 1962, 1963, 1968, 1971, 1972, 1973, 1975, 1977, 1995
by The Lockman Foundation. Used by permission.

Interior design by Sherri L. Hoffman

Library of Congress Cataloging-in-Publication Data

Bower, Christy, 1968-
Best friends with God : falling in love with the God who loves you
 / Christy Bower.
  p. cm.
ISBN 978-1-57293-372-9
1. Spirituality—Biblical teaching. I. Title.
BS680.S7B695 2010
248.4—dc22   2010007281

Printed in the United States of America

Third printing in 2011

Contents

*May the Lord direct your hearts into the love of God
and into the steadfastness of Christ.*

2 Thessalonians 3:5

ONE

God Sends His Love

The Emmaus Travelers

*But God demonstrates His own love toward us, in that
while we were yet sinners, Christ died for us.*
ROMANS 5:8

I went for a long time, years really, where I couldn't perceive
God's love for me. In my quest for answers, I often asked my
pastor, "How do I know that God loves me?" My pastor always
came back to the fact that Christ died for me. While that
answer was true, it wasn't particularly satisfying. Christ died for
everyone else, too. God loved "the world," but did He love *me*?

If you have ever wondered, as I have, if God loves you,
you know that His love can seem distant and impersonal. We
know that somewhere "out there" God loves us, but here and
now we struggle to feel God's love for us. We tend to think
of God loving "the world" as in John 3:16. By extension, we
acknowledge that we are included in that set, though it seems
impersonal. We know that Christ died for us, but He died for
everyone else too.

Seeking an answer to my question, I immersed myself in
the study of God's Word, looking up every verse about God's

love. But while I learned *about* God's love, I still didn't *feel* it. I could see how God interacted with different people in the Bible so I knew that God loved Abraham, Moses, and David, but did He love *me?* Then I began to realize that God did not just love them as part of the collective, "the world," but as individuals. His love was demonstrated in the unique relationship He had with each of them. God interacted in specific ways to respond to their situations: to ease their doubts, to give them faith and courage, or whatever they needed as an individual.

God wanted to respond to me in the same way. I began to bring Him my doubts, fears, heartaches, and problems. As God responded in specific ways, relating to me personally, I no longer felt that God loved me only as part of the collective. God didn't just love the world; He loved *me.*

The question "What's God done for me lately?" might seem like self-centered ingratitude, but perhaps it expresses the deepest longing of our heart to be in a relationship that is personally relevant and dynamic. We don't want a "once upon a time" story about what God did for us two thousand years ago; we want to experience a dynamic relationship with God on a daily basis. We want a page-turner that keeps us engaged from beginning to end with love, drama, constant action, and ever-present hope in spite of impossible circumstances.

Still, in order for us to experience a dynamic love story today, we must go back two thousand years ago to the events of the cross that made our love relationship with God possible. Two men walking home from Jerusalem discussed the unfolding drama that occurred during the Passover. Jesus, whom they had hoped to be the Messiah, had been crucified, and now there were rumors of His resurrection. On the way, a fellow traveler, a man they didn't immediately recognize, joined them

and explained all the things the Scriptures said conce
the Messiah. The events of this journey are recorded in
24, and while we don't know the details of the travelers' dialogue, we do know that they discussed the various promises of
God in the Old Testament regarding the Messiah He would
send. Like the Emmaus travelers, we will see how the events of
Christ's death and resurrection make it possible to experience
a dynamic relationship with God on a daily basis.

To Emmaus and Back

"Mary seemed convinced that Jesus has risen from the
dead, but I'm not sure what to think," Cleopas said to Hebab
as they walked the seven miles from Jerusalem to Emmaus.

"I've known you and Mary for a long time. I've never
known her to tell a lie," responded Hebab. "Still, the idea of
someone dying and coming back to life is difficult to believe.
And if Jesus is alive, where is He?"

"Everyone in Jerusalem seems to be looking for Jesus—
or His body. The Romans who were guarding the tomb are
looking for someone to blame. I fear things could escalate
into riots or even arrests. I am worried about Mary's safety,
but she wanted to stay with the other women a few more
days," said Cleopas.

"Fear not, Cleopas. The disciples will look after your wife
until you return."[1]

Hebab and Cleopas looked over their shoulders at the
sound of hastened strides behind them. "Pardon me," said the
man who approached, "but I was walking a short distance

---

1. Mary the wife of Cleopas was one of the women at the cross (John
19:25), and Cleopas was one of the Emmaus travelers (Luke 24:18).

behind you and heard you mention riots and arrests. Please tell me what is going on."

The three men stopped in the road, and the newcomer saw the sadness in their faces. Cleopas answered, "You must be the only one visiting Jerusalem who doesn't know the things that have happened."

"What things?" asked the man.

Cleopas explained, "There has been a prophet among us, Jesus of Nazareth, who did many miracles. We all hoped He was the promised Messiah who would take the throne of David and overthrow the yoke of Roman occupation. However, the Jewish priests and Roman authorities sentenced him to death. He was crucified three days ago."

Hebab continued with a bit of excitement, "This morning, the women among us went to the tomb to prepare Jesus' body, but the tomb was empty. The women say an angel told them Jesus has risen from the dead and is alive. Some of our men confirmed that the tomb was empty. We searched all day and could not find Jesus. If He is alive, we do not know where He went. The Romans claim the body was stolen, but they were guarding the tomb and as yet have no idea who took the body or how."

The newcomer did not appear to sense the gravity of the situation. "You say that I do not know what is going on," he chuckled, "but you must not know what has gone on before. Haven't you heard what the prophets proclaimed about the Messiah in the Scriptures?" Hebab and Cleopas exchanged glances. The newcomer smiled. "We have a long walk ahead of us. I will explain along the way."

As the three men fell in step together, the man began his explanation. "God created Adam and Eve to have a relationship with Him. God walked with them in the garden, and He loved them and they loved Him. After they sinned by disobeying God, they no longer shared God's intimate fellowship. God still loved the human race, but He decided to choose from among them Abraham, from whom God would create a nation of people who would bear His name."

"Yes, yes," said Hebab, "we know about God's covenant with Abraham. We also know that, later, God's covenant with Moses established the basis for the law."

"Indeed, but God's covenants were never about rules. They were about restoring a relationship with God. Throughout history, God's covenant promises contained three elements of divine assurance: (1) I will be your God; (2) you will be my people; and (3) I will dwell in your midst."

"But God's covenant with David included the promise that a descendant of David would rule over Israel forever. Ever since our years of exile, that has not been the case," said Cleopas.

"The promised Messiah was to be from the line of David," interjected Hebab. "We thought that Jesus would prove to be the Messiah who would take the throne of David and reestablish a kingdom."

"That's right," added Cleopas, "didn't Isaiah write that the government would be upon Messiah's shoulders and that He would uphold the throne of David with justice and righteousness from then on?"

"Ah," the stranger responded, "but the Messiah was not meant to rule and reign from an earthly throne. The Messiah was intended to restore relationships with God. Isaiah also wrote that a virgin would bear a child and name Him Immanuel, which means God is with us. The prophets also spoke of a future covenant, a new covenant."

"Jeremiah spoke of a new covenant," said Hebab, "though I cannot remember his words."

The stranger smiled. "Indeed. The Lord told Jeremiah that He would make a new covenant with Israel, for they had broken the old covenant by which God was a husband to them. In this new covenant, the Lord would write His law within their hearts. He promised to be their God, and they would be His people. Does that sound familiar?"

"Those are two of the covenant promises you spoke of," replied Cleopas. "But what about the third one, that God would dwell in their midst? Is that in the new covenant as well?"

"Actually, the new covenant marks a change from God dwelling among them to God dwelling within them. The Lord told Ezekiel about the new covenant, saying that He would give people a new heart and put His Spirit within them," said the stranger.

"Well, I'm not sure what all that means," said Hebab. "Our ancestors worshiped at the temple but remained separate from God lest they be destroyed in their uncleanness. How then can God dwell within us?"

"The purpose of the new covenant was so that the people could know God. This restored relationship was possible because God would forgive their iniquity and forget their sin."

"All this walking and talking has made me thirsty, and we have arrived at my home," said Cleopas. "Please be my guest for some bread and water. You are welcome to spend the night. It's getting late in the day."

After the three men washed, they lounged on the floor. As Cleopas filled their cups, Hebab asked their guest, "You spoke of the new covenant, but what of the Messiah?"

"The Messiah's blood was necessary to ratify the new covenant."

"You speak as if the Messiah has already come," said Cleopas. "Do you believe that Jesus was the Messiah?"

"It is as you say," replied the guest. He took the loaf and said, "Lord, thank you for the fellowship, the hospitality, and the food." Then he tore off a chunk of bread and handed the loaf to Hebab. As Hebab reached for the loaf, the two men saw the stranger's arms for the first time. At the sight of the nail holes in his wrists, Cleopas and Hebab realized their guest was Jesus. Immediately, Jesus vanished from among them.

After a stunned silence, Cleopas said, "We must go back to Jerusalem to tell the others. Hurry, Hebab, gather our things."

Seven Miles to a Better Relationship

The Bible indicates that it was seven miles from Jerusalem to Emmaus. For the two men accompanied by Jesus, it was seven miles to a better relationship with God. Don't you wish it was that simple for us to improve our relationship with Him? Oh how I wish I could give you seven steps in these seven chapters, but you will simply have to take it one step at a time as you walk with God through life. Every journey begins with a single step and continues one step at a time. You will travel your own unique road through life, but you will not travel alone. God will be with you every step of the way.

The man walking with the Emmaus travelers, whom they would later recognize as Jesus, explained the Scriptures to them so they gained an accurate understanding of God's plan. After they recognized Jesus they said, "Were not our hearts burning within us while He was speaking to us on the road, while He was explaining the Scriptures to us?" (Luke 24:32). The travelers' encounter with Christ touched both their heads and their hearts in a dramatic way.

The way Jesus dealt with the two men demonstrated that He was equally concerned with developing the hearts and minds of His followers. As we walk with Jesus in our own relationship, we must possess both an intellectual assessment of the truth of God's Word and a heart fully engaged in a relationship with God.

I think many people find it easier to gain a mental awareness of God's love than to experience God's love in their heart. Sometimes people will talk about the 12-inch gap between their head and their heart, meaning that they know something with their head but don't feel the reality in their heart. For many years, that's how I felt about God's love for me. I knew in my head that God loved me, but I wanted to feel the reality of God's love in my heart.

Unfortunately, when I could not perceive God's love for me, I ran away from God for a few years. As God began to restore my relationship with Him, I reached a point of knowing that I had to make a decision about whether I would believe that what God said was true. God's Word said that He loved me, but I couldn't see the evidence in my own life. I was almost challenging God to "prove it." In a way, I needed to know that I could trust God.

It was one of the hottest summers on record, so I went down to the coolest part of the basement with my Bible, a huge concordance, a notebook, and a stack of index cards.

I spent the entire weekend looking up every verse on God's love, faithfulness, and other attributes. I learned a lot about God that weekend. What started as a philosophical debate with God somehow touched my heart enough that I surrendered and made a decision to stop resisting God.

As I walked with God, I began to grow in my relationship with Him, but I continued to battle chronic depression. A wise Christian woman urged me to begin keeping a gratitude journal. She encouraged me to keep a notebook by my bed and to record three things for which I was thankful before turning out the lights. She said that by dwelling on positive things before bedtime, I would sleep better. She challenged me to do this for ninety days, suggesting that it would give me a more positive outlook on life.

I took the challenge. At first I recorded obvious and generic things such as being thankful for friends and family. Then I began to pay closer attention to things throughout the day and I discovered many things for which I could be thankful: a compliment from someone that lifted my spirits or a thunderstorm that reminded me of God's awesome power. The exercise forced me to become observant. It increased my awareness of the small ways in which God expresses His love toward us every day.

I maintained the journal for only three months, but it changed my outlook forever. I began to look for and find God's overtures of love toward me in a multitude of small ways. Taking notice of small things opened my eyes to bigger things God was doing in my life. I began to feel grateful that He had healed me from chronic depression, and I marveled at how He had changed my attitude toward Him from one of desperate defiance, like a hurt animal, to one of quiet acceptance and eager anticipation. Or, to put it a different way, I went from being desperate for a drop of God's love to swimming in the ocean of God's love. Finally, I was floating with total confidence in God's love rather than fighting it like a drowning person.

Keeping a list of things for which I could be thankful seemed like a mental activity, but it changed my heart. The mind and the emotions work together in mysterious ways, but it takes both to have a satisfying and well-balanced relationship with God.

The Message of the Cross

Lovingkindness. For years, I had rushed past the word with puzzled indifference. Not only does the word *lovingkindness* seem archaic, but it's a strange compound word. Isn't all love expressed in kindness, and isn't all kindness a loving gesture? To me, *lovingkindness* seemed as redundant as saying "loving-love" or "kind-kindness."

My professor described lovingkindness as "one of the most significant words in the Old Testament." He defined it as loyal devotion or steadfast love. Then he became teary-eyed as he described God's lovingkindness as "a precious treasure not to be taken lightly." It was his depth of feeling more than his definition that caught my attention.

One scholar describes lovingkindness as "the attitude of love which contains mercy." Mercy is withholding from others the reproof that they deserve. Another scholar says, "It is a word which, perhaps better than others, reflects the meaning of the [New Testament] term 'grace.'" Grace is giving others the good that they do not deserve.

Therefore, God's lovingkindness involves withholding from us the punishment that we deserve and extending to us the good that we do not deserve. This doesn't mean that God is soft on sin. Quite the contrary, there is a price to be paid, and He was willing to pay the price personally to rescue us. God's Son took on human form and sacrificed His life to save ours. That's the message of the cross: "God demonstrates His own love toward us, in that while we were yet sinners, Christ died for us" (Romans 5:8). That's lovingkindness.

So, yes, when my pastor would repeatedly point to the cross as evidence of God's love for me, he was absolutely right. Still, sometimes the gift of God's Son seems like getting a vacuum from your husband for Christmas. We want something personal from God. For this reason, salvation—like a gift we aren't sure we wanted—can seem like a nice gesture on God's part, but we aren't sure what to do with it. We tend to leave it on a shelf somewhere as a reminder of the gift that God gave us. Then we go on with our lives as usual. However, salvation is a gift to be used here and now, each and every day. Salvation isn't a free ticket to heaven; it's an invitation to a relationship that produces abundant life.

The Hebrew word *hesed*, which is often translated in English as "lovingkindness," occurs nearly 250 times in the Old Testament. One notable instance occurs when God laments the unfaithfulness of His people and then promises to restore their relationship:

> *I will betroth you to Me forever;*
> *Yes, I will betroth you to Me in righteousness and in justice,*
> *In lovingkindness and in compassion,*
> *And I will betroth you to Me in faithfulness.*
> *Then you will know the Lord* (HOSEA 2:19–20).

Clearly, God portrays himself as a lover. His relationship to His people is described as a wedding vow. Despite the unfaithfulness of His bride, He will remain faithful and extend lovingkindness to her. Isn't that the kind of relationship we are looking for with God?

Why is it, then, that the message of the cross is often described in cold and sterile terms? God's sacrificial love for us is often explained in judicial terms: We have violated the law of God, and the devil has brought charges against us. God, the righteous Judge, declares us guilty as charged, and the sentence for our criminal violation is the death penalty. Out of love for us, God announces that His Son, Jesus, will pay our penalty so we can live. Jesus died on the cross, guiltless yet convicted as a criminal, to pay our death penalty.

Although this explanation is true, it does not stir our emotions the way a romantic love story might. If God described His relationship with His people in terms of a marriage, then we might best understand God's noble sacrifice on our behalf as a love story. Perhaps then we would realize that God's love is the gift we've always wanted.

A Beautiful Romance

The old silent movies portrayed the dashing hero fighting off the dastardly villain in order to rescue the damsel in distress, who was invariably tied to the railroad tracks with a train racing toward her. As laughable as that may seem in its stereotypical simplicity, engaging love stories usually involve a hero who overcomes difficulty through courageous self-sacrifice. He pays a price, at least in terms of personal risk, and he does so because it is the right thing to do. We value such actions as noble and heroic.

Through their encounter with Christ, the men on the road to Emmaus learned that the crucifixion was not the end of hope; it was the beginning of hope. They thought their Messiah was dead, but they learned that the Messiah's death was a necessary part of God's plan. Christ's heroic sacrifice was not the end of a tragic tale; it was the beginning of a beautiful romance.

Do you remember how it felt when someone of the opposite sex first made advances toward you? As that person indicated an interest in getting to know you more, your excitement grew. That excitable feeling is not love, though it is often mistaken for love. The excitement comes from the hope of love. Each of us longs to be loved. We hope that someday, someone will love us. The hope lies dormant until kindled by overtures of love. "*Maybe this is the one*," we think. A spark of hope is lit.

Once we become aware of God's advances toward us, we feel a flicker of excitement as the hope of love is kindled within our hearts. But the spark of hope has been snuffed out so many times before that we ignore it. We've protected our hearts with a callous shell to keep from getting hurt. "*Love? Prove it*," we think. Love seems elusive and God seems intangible, so how can I really know that God loves me?

During a period of loneliness, I called a friend and expressed my desire to feel loved. When she answered the phone I said, "I just want to feel like someone thinks I'm special." Then I burst into tears, and she listened to me cry for an hour.

Doesn't love make us feel special? Whether it was a grandparent who gave us lots of time and attention or the teacher who made us feel like we were her favorite student, love makes us feel special. When a person loves us enough to commit the rest of his or her life to us, we feel special because that person chose us above all others to be his or her lover. That's the way God relates to us. He chose us to be His lover.

After crying on the phone for an hour with my friend that night, I went to sleep exhausted. The next morning I received a card in the mail from a friend in another state. When I opened the card, it said, "God thinks you are special... and so do I." The tears flowed again, except this time they were tears of comfort and joy. Only God could have orchestrated that. The card had been postmarked a few days earlier. It was from a friend who had no idea how I felt, and the timing was perfect. It was a powerful demonstration of God's love for me as an individual. I still have that card, years later, because it was sent special delivery from God through my friend.

God is not perched up in heaven looking down upon the world with a generic sort of love for humanity as a whole. God interacts with us in ways that indicate His unique love relationship with each one of us. He loves us personally and intimately, like no other person can love us.

If we begin to pay attention, we will notice God's gestures of love toward us. He showers us with tokens of His love and waits for us to notice. Like a trail of anonymous love notes, God's blessings lead us to Him. God doesn't want to force us to love Him. That wouldn't be love at all. Still, He faithfully demonstrates His love in our lives, and He waits for us to respond to His love by loving Him in return. He hopes to enjoy a love relationship with each one of us.

God sends His love. He sent His love two thousand years ago by heroically sacrificing His Son's life for ours. He continues to send His love each and every day. God's gestures of love toward us as individuals are intended to get our attention and win our hearts. I hope you begin to anticipate and recognize God's demonstration of love toward you each day.

STUDY QUESTIONS

1. Read about the Emmaus travelers in Luke 24:13–35. What details indicate that their encounter with Christ touched both their hearts and minds?

2. Write down three things for which you are thankful. Consider keeping a gratitude journal for ninety days. What do you think would change in your life if you did?

3. Define God's lovingkindness and describe how it relates to the cross as evidence of God's love for you.

4. What is the difference between mercy and grace? How does Christ's death on the cross demonstrate both?

5. Is God's gift of salvation just a means to eternal life? How is Christ's death a gift to be used each and every day? That is, what did Christ's death make possible for us to enjoy?

6. In Hosea 2:19–20, how does God portray His relationship to His people? What does that tell you about the kind of relationship God wants to have with you?

7. Have you ever had a personal experience that makes you feel certain that God loves you as an individual? If so, describe your experience.

TWO

He Loves Me, He Loves Me Not
The Prodigal's Brother

How great is the love the Father has lavished on us,
that we should be called children of God!
1 JOHN 3:1 NIV

After salvation, the first step on the journey to becoming best friends with God is to believe that He loves you. But many of us, especially when we are new believers, find ourselves wondering how we can know that God loves us. Even if we believe God loves us, we struggle at times. Our emotions swing like a pendulum, alternately believing and questioning God's love for us. While we may have a mental acknowledgment or belief that God loves us, we need some affirmation of it in our lives. But what kind of affirmation do we seek? Emotions can fluctuate wildly, so are they a reliable indicator of God's love for us or our love for God?

Jesus told the parable of the prodigal son to illustrate God's love for us. While we tend to focus on the father and the prodigal son in the story, there is another character that plays a crucial role for the point Jesus is making. The older brother questions his father's love for him.

To give us a fresh look at this familiar story, I've told it from the older brother's perspective while remaining true to the details found in Luke 15. Let's take a moment to immerse ourselves in the story, for we've all probably shared the older brother's feelings at one time or another.

The Prodigal's Brother

It wasn't the sun beating down on his neck that bothered him nor was it the ache in his back or the sting of fresh blisters on his hands from plowing the fields. Instead, he was concerned about his father, who had aged so much in the past few months. Father moved slowly now, with more of a shuffle than a stride. He was becoming stooped in the shoulders, and his face was drawn with worry.

As the oldest son, he was pleased to take over the daily operations for his father. The young man paused a moment to stretch his back and gazed across the field, watching his father pretend to check the foliage in the grape vineyard. Drought and famine had destroyed the crops. For months now, Father had only superficially tended the vineyard.

Beyond concern about the famine, Father had every right to be distraught. His youngest son had essentially said, "I wish you were dead, but you're not, so give me my portion of the inheritance, and I don't ever want to see you again." To everyone's surprise, Father calculated his net worth and distributed half of it to the young man, who took the money and ran.

Father had not heard from his younger son in months, but twice a day, morning and evening, he made a slow, sweeping circle around the vineyard as an excuse to watch the horizon in every direction. *Poor old man. His son would never return.*

The older son resumed work plowing the field. His thoughts turned to his brother. *How dare he essentially steal that money from their father!* A friend had returned from a business trip and reported that the young man was living large in a distant town. Apparently he had gone on a spending spree for himself and was seen giving lavish gifts to women of questionable backgrounds. It angered the older brother to think of his younger brother squandering their father's money with loose living.

Stirred from his thoughts by a commotion, he looked up. His father, who had shuffled around for the past few months, was sprinting across the field. Dropping the plow, he shielded his eyes from the sun for a better look. There in the distance was a figure, with the stature, posture, and stride of his brother. *You've got to be kidding. What's he doing here? If he came back for more money, I'll take him out to the threshing floor and teach him a thing or two. After all he's done to this family, how dare he show his face here again?* He picked up the plow and goaded the ox with the fury that welled up within him. Angry thoughts propelled him forward, furrowing the fallowed ground with a fresh burst of energy.

Hours later, well after dark, the older son returned to the house. The smell of beef roasting over an open fire reminded him of how hungry he was, but he had no intention of eating. The sound of music and gaiety grated on his nerves. *How could Father throw a party like this for a son who had stolen half of his wealth?*

A servant spotted the older son sulking outside. Moments later, Father emerged and said, "Where have you been? Your brother has returned home! Can you believe it?"

"No, I can't believe it, Father. I can't believe you would so easily forgive him after all he's done to this family. You should have kicked him off the property, but instead you threw a party for him."

"My son, come inside and join us. You'll feel different once we are all together again as a happy family."

"I won't set foot in there."

"Okay, let me have a servant bring you some food. You'll feel better after you eat something. You've been working too hard. I know it's been hard for you ever since your brother left."

"I won't eat the food either, not tonight. I can't believe you killed the fattened calf for him. I've worked for you for years. I've done everything you asked and more, especially in recent months as I've accepted responsibility for the family business and dealt with the drought and famine that have destroyed our vineyards and grain fields. After all I've done, you've never thrown a party for me and invited my friends. Why now? Why for him? It's just not fair. You love him more than you love me. In fact, you must not love me at all. Maybe I'm the one who should leave."

"Son, do not sulk because I have been generous with your brother. Months ago, I gave him what he asked for because I love him, as I love you. I forgave him because I love him, as I love you. Tonight we celebrate because I love him, as I love you. He was gone and I thought he might never come back, but you have always been with me. I have always loved you, more than you could possibly imagine. All that is mine is yours. You could have thrown a party at any time and I would take great pleasure in it, because all of this is yours to use as freely as it is mine to give. Do you understand that? Look around you, son. All that is mine is yours."

Pity Party

Have you ever had a bad attitude? No? Me either. Of course we have bad attitudes from time to time. Sometimes we need a new perspective to change our attitudes. It's difficult to rejoice for a repentant brother when you're the one plowing the fields, don't you think? I can see the older brother's perspective. He served his father faithfully while his younger brother spent his inheritance on a life of luxury and loose living. Then, when the money ran out, the prodigal came home. What's worse, their father threw him a welcome home party! When his father tried to offer his perspective on the situation, the older son wouldn't listen. He was miserable and wanted to stay that way. Sound familiar? I thought it might.

The older son's faithfulness over the years was commendable, and he knew it. That was the problem. He told his father, "Look! For so many years I have been serving you and I have never neglected a command of yours; and yet you have never given me a young goat, so that I might celebrate with my friends" (Luke 15:29). While the real party was in progress, the older son stood outside—alone—having a pity party. Even a loving father was an unwelcome guest at this party of one.

Perhaps we are not so different from the prodigal's brother. We serve God faithfully for years, and maybe it seems like someone else gets all the attention. We may begin to wonder, *What about me? Doesn't God love me?* When we begin to develop a bad attitude, we may find ourselves keeping God at arm's length. We implore God, "Show me that you love me!" but we won't let Him close enough to do so.

I didn't realize it at the time, but I used to live in a protective bubble that kept others—including God—a safe distance away. This was more than having "thick skin" so that offenses wouldn't hurt; this was more like an armored tortoise shell. I withdrew into the safety of my shell and wondered why I felt lonely and unloved. I wanted God to prove that He loved me, but I wouldn't let Him past my shell.

I remember one conversation that proved enlightening for me. I confided in someone that I didn't have any friends, just acquaintances. She said, "You don't have any friends because you won't let anyone get to know you. You relate to people only on a task level. You need to let people get to know who you are." I found her observation to be shocking, but true. I wasn't a mean, reclusive ogre. I communicated with co-workers, customers, and people at church, but I was "all business" in my interactions. Her comments gave me the first clue about how to "burst my bubble." I began to poke my head out of the shell a little more often so that others could get to know me. Before long, I discarded the shell altogether and discovered the unexpected result of letting God get closer too.

As in my case, people are seldom aware when they develop subtle defense mechanisms that turn out to be counter-productive, so let's consider some attitudes that tend to keep God at arm's length.

An attitude of defiance. I've already mentioned that I had a defiant "prove that you love me" attitude. I was desperate for God's love, but I wouldn't let Him close enough so that He could demonstrate His love in ways that were meaningful to me. I gradually learned to let God closer by admitting my need for Him.

An attitude of pride. One of the most common ways of keeping God at a distance is a self-sufficient attitude that says, "I can do it myself. I don't need God's help." God can't show us that He loves us if we never give Him the opportunity. We overcome our pride by humbling ourselves enough to ask for God's help. When we admit our need for God, He shows up to meet our need and demonstrate His love for us.

An attitude of presumption. This problem relates to our expectations. We might set all our hopes on asking God for a particular result, and if He doesn't respond as we had hoped, we might presume that God doesn't love us. I used to feel perplexed about how God would demonstrate His love to me. After all, it's not like God can give me (or anyone) a hug. It took me awhile to realize that God might prompt someone to give me a hug when He knew that I needed it. I may have had some wrong expectations. There might have been a bit of presumption on my part that expected God to respond to me in a certain, perhaps unrealistic, way. I understood how humans demonstrate love, but God was intangible, so I wasn't finding evidence of God's love because I didn't know exactly what I was looking for. Once I started keeping a gratitude journal, I began to recognize the subtle ways that God demonstrates His love for me.

An attitude of self-pity. When I locked myself in a protective shell, I was convinced that no one loved me, not even God. Self-pity whispers, "I am unlovable" or, "I am not worthy of love." I know the self-inflicted pain of self-pity, but if you give God a chance, He will prove otherwise: you are lovable and God loves you. We can begin by admitting to God that we need to know His love for us and asking Him to pour out His love in our hearts (Romans 5:5). When we invite God to come into our "bubble," we are one step closer to experiencing His love in our lives.

An attitude of rebellion. In many ways, this begins with an attitude of pride but goes beyond self-sufficiency to self-indulgence. This is the attitude that says, "I'll do it my way. God can't tell me what to do." With an attitude of rebellion, we willfully indulge in sin and tell ourselves that "I deserve this" or even "God would want me to be happy." Clearly, rebellion is the extreme opposite of admitting our need for God. Sin separates us from God, so rebellious attitudes and behaviors, by nature, keep God at a distance. The remedy here is to confess our sins to God so that we may receive forgiveness and restore our relationship. The Bible says: "If we confess our sins, He is faithful and righteous to forgive us our sins and to cleanse us from all unrighteousness" (1 John 1:9). Sometimes it is too much of a leap to go from willful rebellion to confession, so perhaps we can begin by admitting that we need God's help to see things from His perspective. One way to help change our perspective is to remember that Christ was nailed on the cross because of the need to satisfy God's wrath against our rebellious attitudes, as it is written in Isaiah 53:5: "He was pierced through for our transgressions [rebellions], He was crushed for our iniquities [perversions]."

An attitude of independence and isolation from others. It may seem like this has little to do with our relationship with God, but God often answers our prayers and meets our needs through those around us. For example, God demonstrated His love and provision for me through the person who gave me some grocery money while I was unemployed. If we remain distant from meaningful human relationships, it makes it more difficult for God to bless us through others. I've overcome my protective bubble problem, but I still tend to be somewhat reclusive. Writing is a solitary activity, so I have chosen a retail job because I need the social interaction

I have with customers and co-workers in order to maintain a balanced life.

An attitude of independence and isolation from God. If we want to get closer to God, we need to create opportunities to do so. We need to spend time with God by talking to Him about the things going on in our lives, by reading His Word with an openness to what He might teach us, and by making God part of everything we do and increasing our awareness of His presence throughout our day. Be sure that God knows He is a welcome guest in your life at all times and not just in a time set aside for prayer.

Let God Love You

When the prodigal's brother exhibited stubborn self-pity, his pride kept him from experiencing the father's affirmation of love toward him. Likewise, our self-centered attitudes keep us from experiencing more of God's love. Pride says, "I can do it myself. I don't need your help." We cannot enter into God's salvation until we admit our need for God, so it makes sense that our relationship would continue with an ongoing admission of our need for God. The more we see God meet our needs, the more we sense His love and care for us in a meaningful way. Over the course of time we gain confidence in His faithful love towards us.

Jesus told a parable of a religious leader and a tax collector praying in the temple (Luke 18:9–14). The religious leader prayed, "God, I thank you that I am not like other people: swindlers, unjust, adulterers, or even like this tax collector. I fast twice a week; I pay tithes of all that I get." This prideful man was really saying, "I can do it myself. I don't need your help." By his attitude, the religious leader kept God at a distance. On the other hand, the tax collector prayed, "God, be merciful to me, the sinner!" The tax collector admitted his need for God, opening the opportunity for God to meet his need and demonstrate His love.

Bringing our needy hearts to God creates a two-way blessing. It allows God to demonstrate His love for us by giving us what we need, but God also feels loved by us because we trusted Him and came to Him for help. We recognize this two-way blessing when a child is driven by fear to run to his mother for security. In that moment, the mother loves the child and feels loved by him because the child did not come out of obedience but because he trusted his mother to give him what he needed.

One day my sixteen-month-old nephew picked up my flashlight, so I turned it on. The blinds were closed to keep out the afternoon sun, so the room was just dark enough to see the light. Squatting down beside him, I turned him around to face the wall and moved the light around so he could see what the flashlight did. When he saw the light moving around on the wall, he jumped into my arms in fear. It was a spontaneous and tender moment that delighted my heart. He couldn't have said that he loved me more clearly than he did by acknowledging that he felt safe with me.

We try to make God's love complex, but it's really quite simple. We experience God's love for us by letting Him meet our needs, and we demonstrate our love for God by letting Him meet our needs. So instead of keeping God at arm's length, let God love you by admitting that you need Him. This simple act of humility removes the pride that prevents us from experiencing God's love. Admitting your need for God will burst your bubble, as it did mine.

You Have Always Been with Me

I have heard countless sermons on the parable of the prodigal son: God welcomes repentant sinners with open arms. Not only does the father seem to overlook the older brother and celebrate the young rebel, but so do the preachers. I've always felt uncomfortable during such messages because I identify with the prodigal's brother. After all, the father's joy over the returning prodigal didn't seem fair to the responsible son.

In the same chapter as the parable of the prodigal son, Jesus shares another parable that I used to find disturbing (Luke 15:1–7). Jesus describes a man with a hundred sheep, but one sheep gets lost so the man looks for the missing one. When he finds it, he returns to rejoice with his friends. Jesus concludes, "I tell you that in the same way, there will be more joy in heaven over one sinner who repents than over ninety-nine righteous persons who need no repentance" (Luke 15:7).

On the surface it seems as if God overlooks those who remain faithful. With my own sense of indignation, I would echo the sentiments of the prodigal's brother, "Look! For so many years I have been serving you and I have never neglected a command of yours; and yet you have never given me a young goat, so that I might celebrate with my friends" (Luke 15:29).

For years I identified with the prodigal's brother and felt his frustration so much that I really didn't listen to what his father said to him. The father's response seemed disappointing, because all I heard was the father urging him to be glad and celebrate for the brother who was lost but now found.

Listen carefully to what the father says: "Son, you have always been with me" (Luke 15:31). For years, I shrugged with indifference at those words. *Yeah, I have been with you doing all the work, so why aren't you happy with me, too?* No. Listen again: "You have always been *with me.*" God, our Father, rejoices over a repentant sinner, but He takes just as much joy in being with us. Isn't that what the father is saying? His explanation to his troubled son demonstrates the balance between the two. On one hand, we had to celebrate for your brother, but on the other hand, you have always been with me. Both things give the father joy.

If you want God to rejoice over you the way the father rejoiced over his repentant son, then spend time with Him. Make God part of everything you do during the day. Talk to God about your attitudes, your daily activities, and everything you would discuss with your best friend. Spend as much time as possible reading the Bible because it is God's love letter to you. See what He has to say. He rejoices over spending time with us just as He rejoices over a repentant sinner.

To be honest, that makes me feel kind of silly for begrudging the party for the repentant sinner.

All That Is Mine, Is Yours

The father's generosity demonstrated his love for both of his sons. When the older son felt unloved and unappreciated, the father reminded him, "All that is mine, is yours." The tragedy in the parable of the prodigal son is not that the younger son took advantage of his father's lavish love and squandered his father's wealth but that the older son never took advantage of it. Likewise, we can take advantage of all that God has for us.

The Bible says "How great is the love the Father has lavished on us, that we should be called children of God!" (1 John 3:1 NIV). God loves us with unrestrained, extravagant love, so let's take advantage of it by abiding in His lavish love for us.

At the beginning of the chapter I indicated that we need more than a mental acknowledgment or belief that God loves us; we need some affirmation of it in our lives. Sometimes we need to be reminded of the ways God demonstrates His love to us so we learn to see them for what they are. Perhaps it's easiest to see that God demonstrates His favor toward us when He gives us something we ask for or, better yet, when He gives us something before we ask for it. He also demonstrates His favor as He teaches, instructs, and provides fresh insight into His Word, the Bible. God also extends His grace when we have an increased awareness of His presence throughout the day.

I think one of the most important, and easily overlooked, means God uses to extend His lavish love to us is through human interaction. God may be prompting hugs, kind words, and expressions of love to encourage you and build you up. When someone has a kind word for me, I thank God for the gesture of His love toward me.

God's acts of favor toward us come as unexpected blessings. While working at the gift shop at the summit of Big Mountain in Whitefish, Montana, I was making conversation with guests by asking them where they were from. In so doing, I met a woman from Grants Pass, Oregon, and I mentioned that I had a friend there. It would have been incredible odds if we even knew the same person, but this woman was best friends with my close friend from seminary. We swapped stories, and I received an update on my friend's life as if she had come for a visit herself. Better yet, I instantly had a new friend in the Lord. We were both filled with joy at our meeting, and I spent the rest of the day elated and thanking God for the unexpected blessing. Circumstances like this can make you feel certain that God loves you as an individual and not just as part of the collective world.

Anything that provides a moment of happiness is a blessing from God, for He has given us all things for our enjoyment (1 Timothy 6:17). So when we see a small flower poking its head up through a crack in the sidewalk, it is God's signature. God has left love notes all around us, if we will begin to notice them. Enjoy God's lavish love as He showers down expressions of love for you. Not a day goes by without some showers of blessings. Learn to identify them for what they are.

Sometimes we look in our hearts and wonder why we don't have an emotional feeling of love in response to God's love. For me, the emotional response of love in my heart began to occur as I learned to recognize God's gestures of love. However, a little bit of caution is appropriate. Emotions can fluctuate wildly, so are they a reliable indicator of God's love for us or our love for God?

The answer is no, and then yes. Emotional maturity is developed. In the early phases of our relationship with God, it is common to have doubts about God's love for us and to experience the corresponding emotional fluctuations. These highs and lows are not a reliable indicator of the reality of God's steadfast love for us or our developing love for God.

This emotional roller coaster happens because we have limited experience with God on which to establish a firm foundation for our faith. As we have more life experience with God—as we see Him meet our needs time and time again—we come to trust Him more, and the distance between the emotional highs and lows evens out. Our experience with

God over time assures us that He loves us and has our best interest in mind. This assurance becomes an anchor that holds us firm in the knowledge of God's love for us so that our emotions level out. As this happens, our emotions become a more reliable indicator of the reality of God's steadfast love for us and our genuine love for Him.

John indicates that confidence in God's love is a process when he uses phrases like "we have come to know" and "love is perfected in us" in 1 John 4:16–17: "We have come to know and have believed the love which God has for us. God is love, and the one who abides in love abides in God, and God abides in him. By this, love is perfected with us, so that we may have confidence in the day of judgment." As the process of gaining confidence in God's love reaches completion, love is perfected in us and casts out the fear that maybe God doesn't love us, as John indicates in the next verse: "There is no fear in love; but perfect love casts out fear, because fear involves punishment, and the one who fears is not perfected in love" (1 John 4:18). Rest assured that you will grow into complete confidence of God's love for you and eventually the emotional fluctuations will all but fade away.

I believe this emotional maturity that develops in our lives brings us to what the Bible calls "abiding." Jesus gave us a powerful metaphor for what it means to abide in Him when He said that we are to be as dependent upon Him as a branch is dependent upon the vine (John 15:1–11). Just as a branch will wither and die if it is cut off from the life-giving flow of sap from the vine, Jesus indicated that "apart from Me you can do nothing" (John 15:5); therefore, we are to "abide in [Christ's] love" (John 15:9). Let's absorb the meaning of this for a moment. Earlier I indicated that when we admit that we need God, He can demonstrate His love for us by meeting our needs. By living in dependence on God, we receive a continual flow of His life-giving resources.

God reminds us to rely on His abundant resources because "all that is Mine, is yours." Instead of doubting God's love for us, we can bask in His lavish love for us.

STUDY QUESTIONS

1. In the parable of the prodigal son (Luke 15:11–32), which character do you identify with? Why?

2. What are some of the attitudes we can have that tend to keep God at arm's length?

3. How does pride keep us from experiencing God's love?

4. When we bring our needs to God, how does this create a two-way blessing?

5. Let God love you by admitting that you need Him. Jot down several areas of your life in which you need God. Take a moment to talk to God about those things.

6. What does 1 John 4:16–18 teach us about gaining confidence in God's love? How does this relate to our emotional fluctuations that cause us to doubt God's love for us?

7. Explain the powerful metaphor Jesus used in John 15:1–11. How does this relate to experiencing God's lavish love for us?

THREE

Transformed by Love

Paul

The love of God has been poured out within our hearts
through the Holy Spirit who was given to us.
ROMANS 5:5

Once we've settled the matter of God's love for us, we're well on our way to becoming best friends with God. But love goes both ways in a healthy relationship, so how do we grow to love God? As I wrestled with this question, I voiced my concerns to other believers, and more than one person told me, "Act *as if* you love Jesus, and eventually you will." I couldn't see the logic in that. For one thing, isn't that suggesting I should be a hypocrite, pretending to be something I'm not? And, if you will allow me to make a point in an absurd way, does that mean that if I act *as if* I'm an airplane, eventually I will fly? Pretending never creates reality.

The reality is that love comes from God, for "God is love" (1 John 4:8, 16). When asked which of the commandments was the greatest, Jesus replied, "You shall love the Lord your God with all your heart, and with all your soul, and with all your mind, and with all your strength" (Mark 12:30). The Greatest Commandment is to love the Lord. It seems a little startling to be commanded to love. How do we get our emotions to obey a command? We don't. Love comes from God (1 John 4:7). So God commands us to do something (love) that we cannot do on our own, but only He can do through us. Sound surprising? Maybe not when you remember that God desires our salvation, which is not something we can do on our own; only God can save us. Our dependence on Him is essential to having a relationship with Him.

Through the life and teachings of Paul, we'll learn how God creates the reality of love in our hearts. Paul, whom we read about in the book of Acts, was raised as a devout Jew and was trained by a famous rabbi until he became a Pharisee—one of the elite religious leaders of his day. Pharisees demonstrated their devotion to God by their strict obedience to the law. To prove their piety, they went beyond what was required in the law and developed an additional set of rules. For instance, they set aside a portion of their income as a tithe to God, but they went to the extreme and also tithed a portion of the tiniest herbs that grew in the garden (Matthew 23:23) to demonstrate that they were not just spiritual, but super-spiritual. External behavior was all that seemed to matter to the Pharisees. They had plenty of religion, but they lacked genuine love toward God. This was the context of Paul's religious training. As a Pharisee, Paul's religious experience would have been characterized by affectation, a pretense designed to impress others. After an encounter with Christ, Paul's life was characterized by true affection for God. His life was transformed by God's love.

Paul Reminisces

"Ananias!" Paul shouted as he ran after his friend.

Ananias turned just in time to have Paul throw his arms around him. "It's so good to see you, Saul!" said Ananias as he slapped his friend on the back. "But I guess most people know you as Paul now. I'll always think of you as Saul because that is what the Lord said to me that day: 'Ananias, go to the house of Judas on Straight Street and inquire for Saul of Tarsus. He has seen a vision of a man named Ananias come to lay hands on him so that he may regain his sight.'"

Paul gave his friend a gentle jab with his elbow as he remembered, "You were nervous about meeting that day. I could hear it in your voice."

"Well, you were notorious for seeking to destroy Jews who professed to believe Jesus was the Messiah, and that included me. You had search warrants and letters of arrest to put Christians in prison. What was I to think? But once I saw you groping around the house in your blindness, with your eyes all scaled over, you seemed more pathetic than dangerous. How are your eyes, anyway?"

"It's difficult for me to read now, and I write in very large letters, but it's the Lord's way of giving me a constant reminder of how He changed me when He met me on the road to Damascus. I'll never forget it," said Paul.

Ananias said, "I remember when Judas answered the door. He asked me to come back later, but I told him that I wasn't there to see him, but Saul of Tarsus. Judas looked puzzled and stammered something about you not being able to see visitors because you were blind. He thought you had been struck by lightning."

"Lightning?" laughed Paul. "Judas was with me on the road and saw the bright light that knocked me to the ground. I guess he thought it was lightning because he didn't see the

Lord Jesus—but he did hear the Lord's voice say, 'Saul, why are you persecuting me?' Even so, Judas refused to believe, and he was almost angry when I refused to arrest the Christians as planned. Poor Judas. He was a devout Jew, as I had been, but his heart was hard toward God. Did he ever come to know Christ after all these years?"

"No," Ananias responded as he shook his head. "Judas is still one of the chief leaders of the synagogue in Damascus. He says he's still waiting for the Messiah that was promised to the Jews, and he's angry that the news about Jesus has spread to the Gentiles."

"I'll have to visit Judas while I'm in town. Does he still live on Straight Street?"

"Yes, but enough about Judas. How is your missionary work going?"

"Oh, I've traveled from the province of Galatia as far west as the provinces of Macedonia and Achaia. The Lord has opened many doors for effective service. With the help of fellow missionaries and local believers, we've established many churches across the region. I always pray for them, and I write letters to them when I can get some help from someone who can see the words."

Ananias smiled and said, "I hear stories about you from time to time. You'll have to tell me about some of your adventures while we have supper at my home. Come with me, my friend."

From the Inside, Out

Love is not a self-attained virtue. No matter how much we try to make ourselves feel love, we simply can't generate feelings of love on our own. The Bible says that love is from

God (1 John 4:7) and that "the love of God has been poured out within our hearts through the Holy Spirit who was given to us" (Romans 5:5). If Paul could have attained love by his own religious efforts as a Pharisee, he would have achieved it, because he was an overachiever for obeying the law and religious traditions.

Prior to Paul's encounter with Christ, he was a Pharisee. During that era, the average Jew held the Pharisees in high esteem, as models of religious virtue. For all outward appearances, Pharisees obeyed the law and their own religious customs, and they taught others to do the same. That's why people were so shocked that Jesus often rebuked the Pharisees, like when He said, "Woe to you, scribes and Pharisees, hypocrites! For you are like whitewashed tombs which on the outside appear beautiful, but inside they are full of dead men's bones and all uncleanness. So you, too, outwardly appear righteous to men, but inwardly you are full of hypocrisy and lawlessness" (Matthew 23:27–28). We can look good on the outside, but it's what's inside that counts. God wants to change us from the inside, out.

After Paul's encounter with Christ, he preached the message that we are not saved by our religious works but by faith in God: "For by grace you have been saved through faith; and that not of yourselves, it is the gift of God; not as a result of works, so that no one may boast" (Ephesians 2:8–9). Paul's entire life as a Pharisee had been devoted to religious service, but that didn't save him. He learned that having a love relationship with God was all that mattered.

Paul wrote nearly half of the books in the New Testament, but perhaps his best-known and most eloquent words are found in his poetic description of love in 1 Corinthians 13.

According to Paul, the Christian life is characterized by faith, hope, and love, but the greatest of these is love (1 Corinthians 13:13). In 1 Corinthians 13:1–3, Paul establishes the importance of love. He begins by saying that we can talk all we want, but without love, we're just making noise (verse 1). Then he says that we can have spiritual gifts and remarkable faith, but without love, we are nothing (verse 2). Finally, he says that we can give all of our possessions to the poor and die as martyrs for God, but without love, it profits us nothing (verse 3).

Let's not miss the significance of Paul's words here. All of our good works profit us nothing if we do not have love. We can use our spiritual gifts in service for God and give our wealth to do God's work and even die for God, but it's all for nothing if we do not have love. That's pretty astonishing, really. It means that we can't just go through the motions and do all the things a Christian is supposed to do and obey God and hope that the emotions will follow, as my friend suggested when she told me to "act as if you love God, and eventually you will." No, it's apparent that love must come first. Love is what motivates our actions, and love comes from God.

In order for God to put His love in our hearts, He must first deal with the condition of our hearts. God says that we have a heart problem: "The heart is more deceitful than all else and is desperately sick; who can understand it?" (Jeremiah 17:9). This isn't just a hardening of the arteries; it's a hardening of the heart itself. We have hardened our hearts as a means of protecting ourselves from being hurt by the sins of others, but our hearts have also become hardened through our own sinfulness. Jesus said, "For out of the heart come evil thoughts… These are the things which defile the man…" (Matthew 15:19, 20a).

It's as if we were born with a heart that is two sizes too small and hard as a rock—like the Grinch in Dr. Seuss's book *How the Grinch Stole Christmas!* The Grinch was mean and cold-hearted until he unexpectedly found his heart changed. It grew three sizes one day, and he had a greater capacity to love. God says He will perform heart surgery for us and replace our heart of stone with a heart of flesh (Ezekiel 11:19–20; 36:26). A heart of stone has no capacity to grow, but a heart of flesh is flexible. God wants to give us a greater capacity to receive His love as He pours out His love within our hearts (Romans 5:5).

Love may not be a self-attained virtue, but we can cooperate with God in the process of changing our hearts. At the moment of our salvation, God gives us a heart transplant, replacing our heart of stone with a heart of flesh, but from that point forward there is also an ongoing process as "our inner man is being renewed day by day" (2 Corinthians 4:16). This highlights the importance of making our hearts available to God day by day so He can change us from the inside, out.

Knowing God

Our relationship with Christ—truly knowing Him— is how we are transformed by love. Paul contrasted his life before and after encountering Christ by saying he had been "a Hebrew of Hebrews; as to the Law, a Pharisee; as to zeal, a persecutor of the church; as to the righteousness which is in the Law, found blameless. But whatever things were gain to me, those things I have counted as loss for the sake of Christ... in view of the surpassing value of knowing Christ Jesus my Lord" (Philippians 3:5–8). All of the religious things

Paul had done were nothing compared to knowing Christ in a personal relationship.

First John 4:8 says, "The one who does not love does not know God, for God is love." This means that once we truly know God, love is a natural result in our lives. (This includes both love for God and love for others, though my primary focus here is on our love for God.) So if love is a natural result of knowing God, it becomes important to get to know God.

We develop a relationship with God the same way we develop a relationship with anyone else: we talk to God through prayer; we listen as God talks to us through His Word, the Bible; and we share life experiences together by remembering that God is with us at all times.

Prayer. Talking to God does not need to be as formal as some people make it. Many Christians set aside a quiet time in the morning for devotions that consist of prayer and Bible reading. If that works for you, fine. Personally, I find it difficult to form a coherent sentence before ten o'clock, so a morning quiet time doesn't work well for me. I don't wake up at the same time every day; I don't eat at the same time every day; and I don't talk to God at the same time every day. To do so would seem unnatural to me. In fact, the Bible doesn't even say to have a quiet time. The biblical model is to spend every moment of every day with God: "pray at all times in the Spirit" (Ephesians 6:18); "we have not ceased to pray for you" (Colossians 1:9); and "pray without ceasing" (1 Thessalonians 5:17). We can talk to God at any time.

In other relationships, you might call, e-mail, or text someone with brief messages as thoughts occur, and we can get in the habit of communicating with God the same way— as the thoughts occur throughout the day. However, in any significant relationship, you will periodically make time to spend together for a more extended conversation. The same applies in our relationship with God. The time of day, frequency, and duration is flexible, as it would be with your best friend.

When I was a young Christian, I used to wonder what to talk to God about. What was the point of telling a sovereign God the things that He already knew? Prayer seemed like a meaningless monologue, so instead of giving God a daily speech, I began to approach Him with a daily Q&A time, bringing my problems to Him and searching the Bible for clear guidance on specific matters. This was how I started to turn my daily monologues into dialogues, and soon I began having ongoing, spontaneous conversations with God about whatever was going on in my life all day long.

As with any relationship, we cannot expect immediate intimacy in the early stages, but in the process of building the relationship, we gradually share deeper and more personal information with each other. Our relationship with God grows in similar fashion.

If you struggle with the routine of having daily devotions or a quiet time, remember this distinction: devotions are a matter of discipline; devotion is a matter of desire. Once I understood the difference between devotions as an activity and devotion as an attitude, I began to spend more time with God than ever before because my focus changed from fulfilling a duty to building a relationship. I was no longer spending time with God because I had to but because I wanted to, more than ever.

The Bible says that God used to speak to Moses "just as a man speaks to his friend" (Exodus 33:11). We can develop a relationship with God in which we communicate as we would with our best friend.

God's Word. I like to remind people that it takes only eighteen hours to read the New Testament or seventy-two hours to read the entire Bible. They respond by saying that I must be a speed reader. No, far from it. In fact, I'm visually impaired. Actually those are the times it takes to read it aloud, and the times are listed on the consumer information for any audio Bible (although different audio versions may vary in length). People are often amazed because the size of the Bible seems daunting. Eighteen hours doesn't seem like much of a commitment when you put it that way. That's just three hours each evening for six days. You could read the New Testament this week, if you wanted to. Or you could read the entire Bible in seventy-two hours. That's about two and a half hours a day for thirty days. You could read the entire Bible this month, if you wanted to.

Wanting to—that's the key, isn't it? As we are learning to fall in love with the God who loves us, perhaps it is useful to think of the Bible as God's love letter to us. Wouldn't you want to read a letter from your Lover? Or would you say, "I'm really busy, so I'll just read the first page and tomorrow I'll read another one"? Remember, devotion is about desire.

Sure, some parts of the Bible are more interesting than others. I have to admit that I'm squeamish about reading descriptions of leprosy and what the priests did with the entrails of sacrifices. Still, the Bible tells us a great deal about our Lover. We can learn from the historical accounts of how God dealt with others, and these passages tell us about His character. Plus, the examples of biblical characters provide lessons we can apply to our lives as we learn to interact with God.

For a healthy relationship to God's Word, we should approach it with the three C's: casual reading, careful study, and Christ himself. Casual reading means looking for every opportunity to read God's Word. When we have a free evening, we can look forward to reading the Bible the way we would read any other good book—just for pleasure. Careful study means that we will follow our curiosity from time to time, and when we wonder about a person, place, or the meaning of a word, we will look it up in a Bible dictionary for an explanation. You'll be amazed at how much more you'll enjoy the Bible if you understand a little about what you're reading. Take ten minutes to follow your curiosity. Finally, we must remember that our relationship is not with the written Word, but with the Living Word, Christ himself. As we become best friends with the Living Word, the written Word becomes more meaningful and more enjoyable.

Shared experiences. When I talk about spending time with God, I mean talking to Him and allowing Him to speak to you through His Word, but I also mean making God a part of everything you do throughout the day. We dramatically increase the amount of time we spend with God when we interact with Him in the midst of everything we do. When you invariably pick the slowest line at the grocery store, talk to God about it instead of being frustrated. Maybe God will prompt you to start a conversation with the person behind you who needs to know Christ. Or maybe God will prompt you to say something encouraging to the cashier, who may feel the stress of having a long line or a difficult customer ahead of you. Simple conversations with God in the midst of everyday circumstances change your attitude and deepen your relationship with God.

After all, we become friends with someone by spending time with him or her in a variety of situations. And when two people spend time together, soon enough each will know how the other reacts in all kinds of circumstances. The more experiences we share with God, the quicker our relationship will deepen as we learn of God's character and how He responds to us.

We initially gain knowledge of God through His written Word, but over time we also gain firsthand knowledge of His love, forgiveness, grace, patience, and compassion as we see God's character for ourselves, demonstrated in a thousand of life's circumstances. After Job's encounter with God, he prayed, "I have heard of You by the hearing of the ear; but now my eye sees You" (Job 42:5). In other words, we can hear about God, read about God, and know about God, but none of that can replace the kind of knowledge we gain from firsthand experience with God.

When I talk about experience with God, I refer to the quantity and variety of circumstances we have shared with God. Those experiences with God develop the intimacy that would occur in any other relationship in which you share an increasing number of experiences. That's how we become best friends with God.

STUDY QUESTIONS

1. The circumstances of Paul's conversion (Acts 9:1–19) were quite dramatic. Describe how you first came to know Christ. How has God changed your life since then? That is, how have you been transformed by God's love?

2. Love is not a self-attained virtue. Where does love come from (see Romans 5:5 and 1 John 4:7–8)? Write out a prayer asking God to give you His love.

3. What is the main point of 1 Corinthians 13:1–3? What motivates our actions?

4. In what three ways can we develop our relationship with God? Which one would you like to develop further in your life?

5. Look up Ephesians 6:18, Colossians 1:9, and 1 Thessalonians 5:17. Based on these verses, what is the biblical model for prayer?

6. It takes only eighteen hours to read the New Testament or seventy-two hours to read the entire Bible. Have you ever considered reading the Bible just for pleasure, the way you would read any other good book—like a good novel that you can't wait to get back to? Why do you think you don't spend more time in God's Word?

7. What are the three C's used in approaching God's Word? Which one seems like an area you might like to improve? What would you do to improve?

FOUR

The Desire of My Heart

Mary of Bethany

No longer do I call you slaves...
but I have called you friends.
JOHN 15:15

After a lifetime of being taught by our culture that we are valued for our contribution, we find it difficult to believe anything else. We even hear the church plea for money, ask for volunteers, and solicit our participation in every conceivable activity it offers. It's easy to get the wrong idea and think that doing these things makes us a good Christian. It simply isn't true.

The Christian life is about *being*, not *doing*. We say, "I *am* a Christian" instead of "I *do* the Christian life." If the Greatest Commandment is to love the Lord (Mark 12:30), then God desires our love more than our service. And while our service can be a gesture of love towards God, it must never take precedent over or interfere with our relationship with God.

Jesus often visited the home of Mary and Martha. These sisters from the town of Bethany were as different as night and day. Martha was the activist, always doing things. Mary was the contemplative sister and could be found worshiping at the feet of Jesus. Whenever others criticized Mary for being impractical in her devotion, Jesus always defended her single-mindedness, so perhaps each of us can learn something from Mary.

Mary of Bethany

Looking around the room, Mary wondered if this was the biggest celebration the town of Bethany had ever seen. It seemed as if the whole town had turned out. After Jesus raised Lazarus from the dead, everyone wanted to come see for themselves. People asked Lazarus what it was like to be dead and wanted to hear the whole story from his own lips. Witnesses wanted to share their story. In fact, everyone had a story to tell today... a story about Lazarus or a story about Jesus. The room was buzzing with energy.

Mary looked at the alabaster bottle in her hands. *Should I do it? Will there be a more appropriate time, a more private moment? Will others think I am showing off for the crowd?* She closed her eyes and drew in a deep breath. The sound of the crowd faded to background noise. She opened her eyes and looked at Jesus. Love moved both her heart and her feet as she traversed the crowded courtyard toward Jesus.

Jesus was reclining on cushions along with Lazarus and their closest friends. Mary knelt before Jesus. Without a word, she broke the seal on the bottle and poured the contents on Jesus' head. As it dripped off of his hair and beard, she caught some of the oil in her hands and began to massage it into His calloused feet.

This was not the first time Mary had been at the feet of Jesus. She recalled the day that she sat at His feet to listen to Him teach His disciples.

"The Father raises the dead and gives them life, but the Son also gives life to whomever He wishes," Jesus said.

The disciples began to murmur, "Raise the dead? Could it be done?"

Mary's eyes remained fixed on Jesus, and as He looked around at the disturbed disciples, He met her gaze. Although such teaching was usually for men only, no one rebuked Mary for intruding on their meeting, for she lived in this home along with Martha, her sister, and Lazarus, her brother.

"Listen up," said Jesus, "an hour draws near when the dead will hear the voice of God's Son and they will live, for the Father gave the Son authority. I'm telling you, an hour is coming in which those in the tombs will hear His voice. At that time, they will come forth. The righteous will have a resurrection of life, and the evil ones will have a resurrection of judgment." To Mary, talk of resurrection seemed so fantastic. It excited her imagination to envision the dead coming forth from their tombs. It was both thrilling and chilling.

Just then, Martha burst into the room. It seemed as if the aroma of fresh bread wafted into the room with Martha, and a light dusting of barley flour on her face and hair testified to her labor. Martha spoke directly to Jesus, "Lord, don't you care? My sister has left me alone in the kitchen. Tell her to give me a hand."

Mary felt her face flush and she wanted to disappear, for all eyes were on her now. She intended to help her sister, but she had lost track of time as she listened to Jesus. Mary stood to go help Martha.

"Martha, Martha," said Jesus, shaking His head back and forth, "you trouble yourself with so many dishes, but only one is necessary, and Mary has chosen the best one of all. It shall not be taken away from her."

Now, as Mary continued to massage the feet of Jesus, the sickly sweet scent of nard permeated the room. Mary noticed that people began to stop talking as they looked around to see where the smell came from. Aware that people were watching her, she hurried to finish her task. She removed the stick that held her hair and shook her head. Long, dark tresses unfurled themselves, and she began to wipe the excess nard from Jesus' feet with her hair.

The fragrance reminded Mary that a few days ago she fell at the feet of Jesus in grief. Her brother was dead, and Jesus was too late to save Him. She cried, "Lord, if you had been here, my brother would not have died." Jesus began to cry too. Together, they went to the tomb.

There was a stone against the entrance of the cave, so Jesus said, "Remove the stone."

Martha said, "Lord, Lazarus has been dead four days. By this time he will stink."

Jesus said to Martha, "Didn't I tell you that if you believe, you will see the glory of God?"

Some men removed the stone. Then Jesus prayed, "Father, thank you for hearing me. I say this so that the people around me may believe that you sent me." Then Jesus raised His voice and commanded, "Lazarus, come forth."

Mary could not move or even make a sound when she saw her brother waddle out of the tomb. Jesus said, "Unbind him." A few seconds elapsed and no one moved, so Jesus said again, "Let him go." Lazarus was completely healed. The only stench was the sickly sweet smell of the nard and other spices they had wrapped around his body.

As Mary finished wiping the feet of Jesus with her hair, she heard Judas Iscariot say, "What a waste. Why wasn't this perfume sold and the money given to the poor?"

Once again Mary felt her face flush, but Jesus took her by the hand and said to Judas, "Leave her alone. You can help the poor whenever you want. She poured this perfume on my body to prepare me for burial. What she has done will be remembered wherever the gospel is preached in the whole world." With that, Jesus squeezed Mary's hand and nodded at her. She bowed her head, then stood and realized that the room was silent and all eyes were on her. She might have been inclined to run out of the room, but Jesus had just honored her with His words. Mary stood tall, and her long flowing hair made her seem taller still. She paused and looked around the room. Then she glided across the floor with the poise proper for a woman highly esteemed.

Don't You Care?

Martha extended hospitality by welcoming Jesus into her home. She was focused on Jesus until her attention shifted, pulled away by the labor she felt was necessary. It's likely that she was providing food and accommodations for the twelve disciples and perhaps other guests. This was no small undertaking, and there was plenty to do—cleaning house, preparing bedding, and cooking meals. Soon this gracious hostess became grumpy.

Perhaps Martha listened from the kitchen, trying to catch as much as she could of the conversation. Her desire to join the others may have become an ember of resentment burning within her. Or, it could be that Martha was embarrassed by Mary's behavior because a woman's place was in the kitchen, not participating in the men's meeting. Maybe Martha felt overwhelmed by her preparations. Whatever Martha had brewing in the kitchen, it was about to boil over. When she couldn't stand it any more, Martha marched into the room with hands on her hips and unleashed her tongue: "Lord, do You not care that my sister has left me to do all the serving alone? Then tell her to help me" (Luke 10:40).

This was the same sentiment expressed by the prodigal's brother when he told his father that he had served faithfully for years. We tend to point to our service and say, "Look at all I'm doing for you. Don't you love me? Don't you care?" The problem occurs when our relationship has suffered because of our service. Serving God is not a substitute for communing with God, as Jesus made clear to Martha. Our relationship with God must not be neglected in the name of service.

If our service lacks joy, we are caught in servitude. Jesus said, "No longer do I call you slaves... but I have called you friends" (John 15:15). God doesn't want our service; He wants our friendship. We can rest in our relationship with God knowing that He loves us for who we are, not for what we do.

Unfortunately, I think too many Christians are caught in servitude, trying to please God or earn God's favor with their service. What they don't understand is that God is pleased with them, regardless of how much they do for Him.

I once attended a women's breakfast, and the speaker's theme was "Have We Done Enough?" She talked about how her grandfather, on his deathbed, wondered if he had done enough for God. It was perhaps the saddest message I have ever heard because we don't have to do anything for God. The Bible says, "For by grace you have been saved through faith; and that not of yourselves, it is the gift of God; not as a result of works, so that no one may boast" (Ephesians 2:8–9). On our deathbeds we don't have to wonder if we've done enough for God.

Those who wonder if they have done enough for God are piling on burdens that God does not ask us to bear. Jesus said, "Come to Me, all who are weary and heavy-laden, and I will give you rest. Take My yoke upon you and learn from Me, for I am gentle and humble in heart, and you will find rest for your souls. For My yoke is easy and My burden is light" (Matthew 11:28–30). Rest. God gives us rest, not chores. God is not an evil taskmaster cracking the whip over us, demanding that we do more. Relax and let God love you.

One Thing Is Necessary

Whenever we feel overwhelmed by our daily tasks, we must ask ourselves, *Is this really necessary?* Jesus said, "Martha, Martha, you are worried and bothered about so many things; but only one thing is necessary, for Mary has chosen the good part, which shall not be taken away from her" (Luke 10:41–42). According to Jesus, the problem was not with Martha's desire to serve but with what she defined as necessary labor. Food was necessary, but a multi-course meal was not. Martha's attention was pulled away from Jesus by her self-imposed definition of serving Him, and her overdone service to Him hindered her spiritually. We can fall into the same trap of going overboard in our service. It's easy to get carried away, adding one thing and then another until we are overloaded. Perhaps the question we should be asking ourselves is, "How much am I trying to do for God that He doesn't require of me?"

I had my own Mary and Martha experience when a friend asked me to help with the women's retreat. We spent Thursday decorating, preparing gift bags for the ladies, and making sure everything was ready. It didn't seem like there was much left to do, so I told the other workers that I would return Friday afternoon, about an hour before registration. My friend called me Friday morning and said, "Get down here as quickly as you can. We need all hands on deck."

I ate an early lunch and arrived around noon. Then I stood around for two hours while the other workers ate lunch. Finally, at two o'clock, I was tasked with hanging signs and Scripture verses on all of the doors. That took an hour. Afterwards, I walked around looking for something to do, but it seemed as if everyone was ready and waiting. I wondered why my friend had thought there was such a crisis. It seemed like there was no need for my presence, so I disappeared for a while. When I returned, my friend anxiously asked, "Where have you been?"

With a sheepish smile I admitted, "I snuck out to my car for an hour to spend time with God. I wanted to prepare my heart for the service tonight." She didn't seem to know what to say to that. I wondered if she had forgotten why we were having a retreat.

The Bible says Mary "was seated at the Lord's feet, listening to His word. But Martha was distracted with all her preparations" (Luke 10:39–40). Serving God is a good thing, until the service becomes a distraction that pulls us away from our relationship with God.

At the retreat that weekend, I watched women scurry about doing all kinds of tasks. For instance, they decorated the tables with different centerpieces and colors for each meal and placed a special craft at each place setting—butterfly magnets for one meal and scrolls at another meal. Not only did women spend hundreds of hours making these crafts, someone had to miss part of the worship or message in order to decorate for each meal. That's the part that bothered me. We came to the retreat to spend a weekend immersed in worship and the Word of God, and so many extra things had been added that it distracted from that purpose.

I began to think about what a retreat would be like if it were prepared by "Marys" instead of "Marthas." At a Mary retreat, everyone would eat before they arrived on Friday night so we could devote the entire evening to worship and the Word of God. On Saturday morning, we would have muffins and fruit so we could get on with the good stuff. For lunch, we would have peanut butter and jelly sandwiches on paper plates so no one would have to spend time preparing food or cleaning up. Our afternoon free time would be spent in additional worship. For dinner we would call out for pizza delivery—again, no cooking, no cleanup—so we could hurry back to worship. On Sunday morning, we would have another continental breakfast before our service began. There would be no tablecloths, no decorations, and no frills. And by contrast, these arrangements are pretty luxurious, because some Marys would avoid the meal problem altogether by fasting.

Most likely, a retreat planned by Marys wouldn't have much appeal for the Marthas. They are so focused on preparations—on doing—that they probably wouldn't be able to enjoy themselves at a retreat that didn't require planning, hard work, and many details. And for a Mary, that is difficult to understand.

During that same time frame, our church was searching for a pastor. A candidate came and proposed all of the programs and ministries he would institute if he became our pastor. It bothered me because I felt that our church didn't need more programs; we needed more of God and God's Word. I wondered: *If church didn't offer opportunities to do things, would the Marthas continue to come?*

The Best Part

At the retreat, when we took our seats at the banquet, the first thing I noticed was dessert. Above each place setting, a dessert plate was drizzled with raspberry sauce and arranged with three small dessert items. "This is my kind of banquet," I announced to the women around me. "Eat dessert first." The main course had not arrived yet, but it looked to me as if they had already served the best part.

Spending time with Jesus is the best part. It's like having dessert first. Mary was "seated at the Lord's feet, listening to His word" (Luke 10:39). When Martha complained about this, Jesus said, "Mary has chosen the good part, which shall not be taken away from her" (10:42). By this He meant that Mary had chosen to sit and listen to Him, and He would not ask her to do otherwise.

I could have looked at the plate before me and said, "It is my duty to consume this dessert." But, to me, eating dessert was not a duty. It was a desire so strong I could barely contain myself. Everything in me wanted to dip my finger in the raspberry sauce when no one was looking so I could sample the good stuff. To me, the duty was in the unnecessary waiting dictated by etiquette. Whether we are motivated by duty or desire affects our relationship with God.

Do you consider spending time with God a pleasure? I'm afraid too many Christians set aside time with God as a

Christian duty. They deem it a spiritual discipline, and discipline isn't meant to be enjoyable, just endured. However, when you are best friends with God, you can't wait to spend time with Him. Time with God is a pleasure, not a chore.

Spending time with God is the best part of my day, so I try to incorporate time with Him throughout my day. It's like sneaking a bite of dessert every chance I get. Psalm 34:8 says, "O taste and see that the Lord is good; how blessed is the man who takes refuge in Him!" Maybe you need to give God another taste test. You'll see for yourself that God tastes good, like having dessert first.

When we first become a Christian, the natural question is: *What do I do now?* This sets us on a path of duty in which things are clearly defined as right or wrong. Duty shapes our behavior but doesn't always shape our hearts. Duty is an obligation, but God doesn't want our relationship with Him to be one of obligation. That's not a loving relationship. However, at least duty is a starting point, and God can work on our hearts as we grow in our relationship with Him. As we become best friends with God, our motivation will shift from duty to desire.

God desires devotion, not duty. If a relationship is reduced to duty, it's not much of a relationship. I have heard many people confess their guilt and frustration at their inability to maintain a consistent and satisfying quiet time. The guilt comes from feeling we have shirked a duty. Nurturing any relationship, especially with the One who loved me enough to die for me, should not be perceived as a duty that breeds guilt. God doesn't want us to feel duty bound to spend time with Him.

Duty says, "I have to," but devotion says, "I want to." Duty does only what is required; devotion seeks to do as much as possible. Duty borders on laziness; devotion borders on lavishness. Duty may try to satisfy a perceived minimum requirement with a daily dose of God, but devotion tries to satisfy an unquenchable thirst for God and an addictive appetite for God's Word. Reading the Bible seems overwhelming when perceived as a duty, but when you love the Author, it is a joy to read it over and over again.

Some people perceive the Bible as a big list of dos and don'ts. God wants our obedience, but He wants it to come from the heart. He said of Israel: "Oh that they had such a heart in them, that they would fear Me and keep all My commandments always, that it may be well with them and with their sons forever!" (Deuteronomy 5:29). God didn't want Israel's legal compliance; He wanted their love and devotion. As we fall in love with the God who loves us, we find our actions motivated by love. We put God's Word into action because we love Him and we want to please Him. We are not driven by duty, but by devotion to pursue the things that will please our Lover, such as being generous, patient, and forgiving.

Mary was not driven by duty, but by desire when she anointed the feet of Jesus with costly perfume. Her extravagant gift of pure nard imported from India was worth a year's wages. Jesus wasn't impressed by the value of the gift, for He had previously applauded a widow who had put into the offering two copper coins worth less than a penny (Mark 12:41-44). And yet, Jesus said of Mary, "Wherever the gospel is preached in the whole world, what this woman has done will also be spoken of in memory of her" (Mark 14:9). Jesus did not commend Mary's act as much as her attitude.

Mary chose the good part by spending time with Jesus while Martha grumbled about doing the chores. On that particular day, Martha may have missed the point, but in fairness to Martha, there is evidence that she chose the good part at other times and sat under the teaching of Jesus, for Martha knew the Scriptures. When she greeted Jesus after Lazarus' death, she engaged in a theological discussion with Jesus. She proved to be well-informed and full of faith. Listen to her three confessions:

- "I know that whatever You ask of God, God will give You" (John 11:22).
- "I know that [Lazarus] will rise again in the resurrection on the last day" (11:24).
- "I have believed that You are the Christ, the Son of God" (11:27).

Martha affirmed Christ's omnipotence; she was knowledgeable about the end times; and she stated her belief that Jesus was the awaited Messiah promised by God in the Scriptures. Women of her day did not receive formal education nor were they able to fully participate in the synagogue, so Martha's knowledge is remarkable. She excelled at more than homemaking. Apparently, she spent time with Jesus and chose the best part on other occasions.

Just as Martha may have missed the point on a particular day but focused on Jesus on other occasions, the planners of our women's retreat came back a year later with a much simpler approach to the weekend. Instead of a stage constructed like the set of a Broadway play, a few scraggly trees hid the sound system. Instead of someone missing the sessions to decorate the tables with different crafts for each meal, someone walked around during the dinner meals to hand out simple keepsakes with Bible verses. Instead of a professional speaker on a book tour, we had the leader of a prayer ministry. The whole event had a more intimate, relaxed feel. The Marys were more comfortable and the Marthas still had things to do, but not to the point of distracting from the main purpose. We easily overburden ourselves, but we can learn to keep our focus on Jesus.

Compelled by Duty or Love

Although I was a faithful Christian involved in church through high school, I drifted away from God and church during my college years. Later, I began to dabble in church again, and within a few months I recommitted my life to Christ. The church processed me as if I had just enlisted. A spiritual advisor began calling me regularly to see if I was reading my Bible and praying; I was put in a class to learn the fundamentals of the faith; and someone called me to assign me to an area of ministry and wanted to know my preferences.

"I'm not interested, thank you," I replied.

"Well, the church can't operate without volunteers to make everything happen, and it's your duty as a Christian to support and serve in your local church. So which area of ministry interests you the most?"

I ended up duplicating and selling recordings of the sermon after each service. After years of being away from God, I needed a period of spiritual renewal, and instead I was plunged into a yoke of duty-bound service. I wasn't serving God because I wanted to; I was serving God because I had to.

Later, someone discovered that I had latent skills as a former French horn player, so I was reassigned to the worship team. This demanded even more of my time, with two rehearsals a week, plus practice time and two or three services. Eventually, I began having panic attacks on Sunday mornings. This didn't seem like the abundant life that Jesus promised.

A wise person took me aside and said, "Christy, there are times when we need to minister to others, and there are times when we need to step back from everything and be ministered to. Do what you need to do. There is no shame in that."

Jesus extends an invitation to you: "Come to Me, all who are weary and heavy-laden, and I will give you rest. Take My yoke upon you and learn from Me, for I am gentle and humble in heart, and you will find rest for your souls. For My yoke is easy and My burden is light" (Matthew 11:28–30). If you are weary and that invitation sounds appealing to you, perhaps you need to take a leave of absence from your Christian service or ministry position. Not only is there no shame in that, I believe it is honorable and commendable for people to take time to focus on their relationship with God without other distractions. Quit doing anything for God, if necessary, until you are fully immersed in a love relationship with God. Focus on the best part.

Years later, I attended a church in which each of the pastors took a month of sabbatical each year (in addition to regular vacation time). They were released from their normal duties so they could study and pray. They were free to attend services at our church or at another local church, if they so desired. It was healthy for them as individuals and for the church as a whole.

If doing Christian things has become more important or more demanding than your relationship with God, then it's time for a spiritual sabbatical. There is nothing that you do for God that is more important than your relationship with God. Doesn't God need our service? Not at all. Paul said that God is not "served by human hands, as though He needed anything, since He Himself gives to all people life and breath and all things" (Acts 17:25).

Once our hearts are filled to overflowing with the love of God, we will be ready to pour out that love in service to God. Let's be compelled to serve by our love for God and nothing else.

STUDY QUESTIONS

1. Describe the contrast between Mary and Martha (see Luke 10:38–42). Which one do you identify with? Why?

2. What is the theme or message of each of these verses?

    Matthew 11:28–30

    John 15:15

    Acts 17:25

    Ephesians 2:8–9

3. Do you feel like your service to God distracts you from your relationship with Him? List the things you do for God and pray about them every day until you are certain which ones God asks of you and which ones are not necessary. Also pray for the courage to make changes as needed.

4. When you are best friends with God, time with God is a pleasure, not a chore. Do you consider spending time with God a pleasure? Or do you see it as a Christian duty or spiritual discipline?

5. Describe the contrast between duty and devotion in our relationship with God.

6. Mary was not driven by duty, but by desire when she anointed the feet of Jesus with costly perfume. As we fall in love with the God who loves us, we find our actions motivated by love. Do you feel that your service to God is motivated by love or duty? Why do you think you feel that way about it? What, if anything, could you do differently?

FIVE

Loving God with Our Lives
David

I love You, O Lord, my strength.
PSALM 18:1

The more life experiences we have with God, the more our love for Him grows and multiplies. Although we can't make ourselves feel genuine love for God, we can't prevent it once we experience God's personal interaction with us. Love grows as a relationship develops. That's the nature of friendship.

As we begin to experience a dynamic relationship with God on a daily basis, we enter into a lifestyle characterized by constant companionship with God. We realize that we are not one of the collective, as if God only loved "the world" in the global sense. Far from it! When God interacts with us in ways that indicate His unique love relationship with us, our natural response will be that of worship and service as expressions of our love. Being best friends with God will result in loving God with our lives.

In the Bible, David was an example of someone who loved God with his life. He had an interactive relationship with God. The Bible tells us a great deal about David's life, so I have narrated three events that illustrate his loving relationship with God. Let's see what we can learn from David about how to love God with our lives.

David and His God

The crisp call of a ram's horn sang through the skies in a long majestic melody. David altered his course to follow the sound. Despite the chill in the air and the morning dew on the grass, David knew that it would be miserably hot soon enough. As he crested the hill, he gasped at the sight of the army of Israel in full battle formation. Three short blasts on the ram's horn were each followed by a responding battle cry from the men. Then the army marched down the Valley of Elah to meet the Philistine army.

David quickly left his parcels at the army outpost and scampered down the hill to catch up to his brothers. As he entered the battle line, he scanned the anxious faces of men, looking for his brothers. When he spotted them, he called out, "Abinadab! Shammah!"

They turned to greet David, slapping him on the back. "Is all well? Is Father well?" they asked.

"Yes, all is well," answered David. "Father sent me with food supplies for you. I left the bags at the outpost for you to pick up later. What's going on?"

"Normally, I would say it is dangerous for you to be here, David," said Abinadab, "but we have been in a stand-off with the Philistines. Twice a day for forty days, the Philistines have sent forth a ten-foot-tall giant to taunt us and challenge us to send forth a man to face him in one-on-one combat."

"Why doesn't someone do something?" asked David.

"Haven't you seen this man?" said a soldier standing nearby. "Here he comes now. They call him Goliath."

David pushed past a few soldiers for a better look. The imposing figure wore a bronze helmet and armor, even on his legs. His spear was the size of a weaver's beam. He shouted, "Why do you come in battle formation if you don't intend to fight? You came to fight the Philistines. I am a Philistine. Fight me. Send over a man to fight me. If he kills me, we will become your servants, but if I kill him, then you will become our servants." The giant paced back and forth and then called out again, "I defy the ranks of Israel to send a man to fight me." Then, he appeared even more menacing when he began to bang his sword and spear against the shield held by his armor bearer.

David watched as the soldiers nearby backed up a bit, and some tried to take cover. "Who is he to taunt the armies of the living God?" said David. "Why hasn't anyone gone out to meet him? Didn't King Saul promise anything to the man who would kill this Philistine?"

David's oldest brother, Eliab, approached for the first time. "What are you doing here?" he scolded. "Your little flock of sheep will wander off if you keep coming down here to watch the battle. Mind your own business."

"What have I done now?" pleaded David. "I only asked a question." David searched the face of Eliab but found no kindness there. Eliab had treated his youngest brother this way ever since Samuel had anointed David with oil, saying that he was the Lord's anointed one.

One of the soldiers said to David, "Come with me." When they arrived at the army camp, David was brought to King Saul. "Don't worry, my lord," said David with a bow. "I will go and fight this Philistine."

Saul began to laugh and then cleared his throat to cover it. "That's very brave of you, but you are just a youth, and this seasoned warrior has been fighting since he was a lad himself."

David said, "Whenever I tended my father's sheep and a lion or a bear came and took a lamb, I pursued him and attacked the beast to rescue the lamb from his mouth. When the beast would rise up against me, I would strike him and kill him. I have killed both the lion and the bear, and this Philistine is a beast like them for taunting the armies of the living God. The Lord who delivered me from the claws of the lion and the bear will deliver me from this Philistine."

"May the Lord be with you," said the king, "for in you we will put our trust, and in the hands of the Lord will be our fate." Then the king outfitted David with his own armor.

Although David had served as a musician in the king's court and even as the king's armor bearer, he had never dared to try on the king's armor. It was enormous, for King Saul stood a head taller than the other men of Israel. David looked silly in the king's armor and could barely move. As he took off the king's armor, he said, "My lord, I am honored at your gesture for the sake of my well-being, but I cannot fight like this."

David set off for the battle line with his shepherd's staff in one hand and his slingshot in the other, with five stones in his shoulder bag. As he approached, Goliath called out, "Am I a dog that you come to me with sticks?"

David replied, "Quit barking at the armies of Israel. You come to me with a sword, a spear, and a javelin, but I come to you in the name of the Lord, who will deliver you into my hands so that everyone will know that the Lord does not deliver by sword or spear. The battle is the Lord's."

Then Goliath lumbered across the field toward David, and David sprinted toward Goliath. David slung a stone toward the giant, and it sank into Goliath's forehead so that he fell to the ground. David had no sword, so he drew Goliath's enormous sword out of its sheath and cut off the giant's head.

The armies of Israel pursued the fleeing Philistines, but David was whisked away from the battle. When David was brought before King Saul, he still held Goliath's head in his hand as evidence that God had given him victory. The God that David came to love and trust in the wilderness while tending sheep had proven himself trustworthy once again.

Years later, when David became king, he never forgot that the Lord was with him that day. After another war with the Philistines, David brought the ark of the covenant to Jerusalem. The ark of the covenant arrived in the city amid great celebration. The procession included musicians and dancers. Shouts of joy filled the air, along with the sound of trumpets, cymbals, harps, lyres, and singers.

King David removed his royal robes and donned the same linen ephod worn by the other musicians. Overjoyed at the presence of the Lord, the king was leaping and dancing before the Lord with all his might. Michal, David's wife, heard the procession approaching and looked out her window. When she saw David's exuberant dancing, she despised him.

After the celebration and ceremonies, David returned home. His wife Michal, the daughter of Saul, met David in the courtyard. "My, how you've distinguished yourself today!" she said with sarcasm. "Is that any way for the king of Israel to behave? You made a fool of yourself today, and instead of acting like a king, you degraded yourself and behaved like a commoner."

The flush of anger burned David's cheeks as he said, "The Lord chose me over your father to be king of Israel. I celebrated before the Lord. I will humble myself in my own eyes, but in the eyes of the people, I will be honored." David loved God and wasn't embarrassed to show it.

Years later, near the end of David's life, after yet another war with the Philistines, David ordered a census to count all of the people of Israel and Judah. As the census was underway, David began to feel guilty about his prideful desire to know the size of his kingdom, so he asked the Lord to forgive him. The prophet Gad brought the Lord's reply to David: "I am offering you three consequences for your pride in counting the people of Israel. Either you shall face seven years of famine in the land, or you will flee three months from your enemies, or the angel of the Lord will bring destruction throughout the land for three days. Make your choice."

David paced back and forth in his throne room, thinking over the choices. At length he said to Gad, "Please let me fall into the hand of the Lord, for He is merciful, but do not let me fall prey to my enemies."

The angel of the Lord slew seventy thousand men of Israel. As the angel was passing through Jerusalem, the Lord said, "It is enough. Stop." The angel was standing by the threshing floor of Ornan the Jebusite, and David saw the angel standing between heaven and earth with his sword drawn and stretched out over Jerusalem.

Ornan was threshing wheat and saw the angel of the Lord. Then he saw King David approaching, so he fell at the king's feet. David said to him, "I want to buy the site of this threshing floor that I may build an altar to the Lord, that the plague may be restrained from the people."

"My lord," said Ornan, "you may have anything you wish. I will also give you oxen and wood and grain for the offering."

David said, "No, I will pay you the full price, for I will not give the Lord an offering that costs me nothing."

So David bought the site and built an altar there. He called to the Lord, and the Lord answered him by sending fire from heaven on the altar of burnt offering. Then, the angel put his sword back in its sheath. David knew this was holy ground, so he designated it as the site for the temple of the Lord to be built. David's love for God inspired great generosity toward God.

Experience with God

One of the joys of attending Sunday school as a child is the opportunity to hear great Bible stories that capture the imagination. What child couldn't imagine slaying giants like David did? It's too bad that as we get older, we get serious and practical. I have to admit that when I was a child, my image of Goliath was that of the Jolly Green Giant that I saw on boxes of frozen vegetables at home. I knew Goliath didn't seem very jolly, so I think my image of him blended a bit with the Incredible Hulk to make him seem scarier. At any rate, to me, Goliath was green.

David was young enough to have some imagination too. When the army of Israel trembled before the mighty Goliath, David saw a puny animal taunting the mighty God of Israel. God was the real giant in David's mind.

As youthful as David was, his personal experiences with God gave him greater confidence in God than the armies and leaders of Israel. This young shepherd boy, who had defended his flocks against wild animals by day and night, said, "The

Lord who delivered me from the paw of the lion and from the paw of the bear, He will deliver me from the hand of this Philistine" (1 Samuel 17:37). David knew that "the battle is the Lord's" (1 Samuel 17:47) because he had experience with God. He knew that God had intervened in his life before, and this was no different.

The people of Israel who faced Goliath that day had been raised in a religious culture. From childhood they were taught the Word of God and participated in the religious ceremonies and festivals prescribed by God. They had followed the God of Israel all of their lives, and yet they lacked the confidence of this boy, David. Why? They knew that God cared about Israel as a nation, but they didn't have their own personal history with God to know that He cared about them as individuals.

This highlights the difference between a corporate relationship with God and a personal relationship with God. It's not enough to grow up in a Christian family or to attend church regularly. While we need a sense of community, we must have a personal relationship that involves repeatedly trusting God with our lives just as David trusted God to defeat Goliath.

We might need to trust God to help us learn to live on a smaller income or to give us insight into how to mend a broken relationship or to help us learn to live with a physical ailment or disability. Even in our day to day lives, we can learn to trust God by bringing every need to Him and letting Him meet our needs. As we see God interact with us in our specific circumstances, we know that He cares about us as individuals. Developing a personal history with God is how our love and trust grow.

Experience with God and years with God are two different things. Someone who has been a Christian for forty years but who crumbles in the face of crisis demonstrates a lack of experience with God. That person lacks the confidence of David, who knew from personal experience that God was bigger than any giant. Experience with God in the past gives us confidence in the present that God will be there for us in the future. We know for certain that "Jesus Christ is the same yesterday and today and forever" (Hebrews 13:8).

But what if you have little experience with God? The Bible is full of examples of how God interacted with people like David. We can have faith that the God who did those things for those people is the same God today. As we trust Him, He responds to us so that we develop our own history with God that is every bit as exciting as the lives of David and others in the Bible.

Interactive Worship

When you think of worship, what do you think of? Most of us think of a time of singing at church. Singing praises to God is part of worship, but, in a larger sense, worship is our response to God. As God reveals himself to us, our natural response is worship. I know one woman who arrives at church just in time for the sermon because she says, "I don't get anything out of the worship." That's the point. We don't get anything out of worship; we give as we worship. As a response to God's great love for us, our hearts well up with love for Him and overflow in spontaneous gestures of our love for God. Those gestures might include singing, giving, serving, or any act that demonstrates our love for God. That's how we love God with our lives.

The Bible makes a distinction between true worship and false worship. Jesus said that "true worshipers will worship the Father in spirit and truth" (John 4:23). True worship is a personal response to God. False worship is obeying pre-scribed rituals without a heart response to God.

During the time of Isaiah, the prophets and priests lead-ing Israel refused to listen to Isaiah's message from God. Instead, the spiritual leaders of the nation mocked God's message and His messenger, Isaiah. Israel continued to follow the sacrifices and rituals prescribed in the law, but they were just going through the motions of following God because they really didn't want to hear and obey Him. For this reason, the Lord rejected their meaningless gestures of worship, say-ing, "This people draw near with their words and honor Me with their lip service, but they remove their hearts far from Me, and their reverence for Me consists of tradition learned by rote" (Isaiah 29:13). We can do all the right things, but if it's mere obedience without a heart response, it's worthless.

Today, some people pay lip service to God by calling themselves Christians without giving their lives to God. They want to associate with God—at least in name—but they don't want God to interfere with their lives. We can't just go through the motions of going to church or calling ourselves Christians. Our relationship with God must play a dynamic role in our lives.

David understood the difference between true and false worship. He said, "Give me the site of this threshing floor, that I may build on it an altar to the Lord; for the full price you shall give it to me, that the plague may be restrained from the people" (1 Chronicles 21:22). Ornan offered to give the king anything he desired, but David said, "No, but I will surely buy it for the full price; for I will not take what is yours for the Lord, or offer a burnt offering which costs me noth-ing" (1 Chronicles 21:24). David did not want to go through the motions of offering a required sacrifice to God; he gave from his heart.

God often rebuked Israel for offering sacrifices that were meaningless. There were laws for prescribed sacrifices to be brought before the Lord, but God didn't need the people's burnt offerings. After reminding them that He owned the cattle on a thousand hills, God said,

> *If I were hungry I would not tell you,*
> *For the world is Mine, and all it contains.*
> *Shall I eat the flesh of bulls*
> *Or drink the blood of male goats?*
> *Offer to God a sacrifice of thanksgiving*
> *And pay your vows to the Most High;*
> *Call upon Me in the day of trouble;*
> *I shall rescue you, and you will honor Me*
> (PSALM 50:12–15).

Consider those pivotal words, for God was trying to shift His people's thinking, and ours, about true worship. God doesn't need anything from us, but He does tell us to offer a sacrifice of thanksgiving, which is a heart response to God. Then God says to pay your vows. That is, do what you say you're going to do. If you say you're going to follow God, then do so without reservation. Finally, God explains the interactive nature of true worship: "Call upon Me in the day of trouble; I shall rescue you, and you will honor Me" (Psalm 50:15). Instead of obeying sacrifices and traditions learned by rote, God says that true worship is interacting with Him. Look at how interactive this is: First, we call upon the Lord; second, He responds to us by meeting our needs; and third, we have a heartfelt response to Him. That is true worship.

Once again, we come back to the very simple premise: we let God love us by admitting that we need Him. When we let God meet our needs, we feel God's love for us, and we demonstrate our love and trust for God. We also experience a heartfelt response to God. The essence of worship is to love God with our lives. That's being best friends with God.

Hearts and Minds

David's first claim to fame, the thing people knew him for, was his aptitude for music. While he was only a shepherd boy, his reputation as a musician brought him to the courts of King Saul, where he played music to soothe the troubled spirit of the king. From these humble beginnings and through his own kingship, David's music undoubtedly soothed his own soul as he poured out his heart to God. For hundreds of years since then, David's psalms have been influential in soothing the souls of others who read them.

Undoubtedly, David felt closest to God through music and prayer. Many people would agree that they feel closest to God while singing songs of worship, especially corporately. Some people prefer the symbolism and orderliness of liturgy as a means of drawing near to God. Some of us may feel closest to God in church, some outdoors, and some in a personal place of prayer. None of these things are right or wrong, and God is pleased to meet us where we are most comfortable meeting Him. We are God's children, and He knows that with each of our different personality types, we will tend to relate to Him in different ways.

I feel closest to God when I'm studying God's Word, with my Bible and several reference books open to relevant sections and spread in a semi-circle on my desk. I relate to God very strongly with my intellect, but my knowledge engages my emotions, too. When I walk away from my desk, I continue to contemplate various truths from God's Word throughout the day or during sleepless watches of the night.

The intellect and the emotions both play a vital role in how we relate to God. While we may lean a bit more toward one or the other, both need to be developed to create a healthy balance. Problems arise when we allow either the intellect or the emotions to dominate our relationship with God.

As I tried to discover how to feel love for God, I realized that I mostly related to God with my mind. I studied the Bible and analyzed God's love, but I didn't know how to feel it or respond to it. That's when I realized that at the other extreme, like the swing of a pendulum, the best we can do to muster a feeling of love on our own is to get ourselves worked up with super-charged emotions, with little substance on which to build a long-term relationship. In human relationships, we call this infatuation.

Infatuation is emotion without reason. We can get so caught up in our emotions that we cease using logic. Sometimes it's difficult to distinguish between infatuation and love because the emotion is there, but infatuation is characterized by foolish or unreasoning passion. Two lovers might feel strongly toward each other, but they have not had enough time together to rationally determine if they are truly compatible. They have not shared enough experiences together to have a relationship in which love has developed. It takes time for love to grow.

Infatuation with God is also characterized by foolish or unreasoning passion. Some people get so caught up in their emotions that they live from one spiritual high to the next.

For them, it's all about experiencing a particular emotional response or manifestation, but they lack the substance on which to build a long-term relationship with God.

In his book *Religious Affections*, Jonathan Edwards addresses the need for balance in our emotions when he writes: "True spirituality must be something more than pure emotion—and yet we cannot be truly spiritual if our hearts are untouched. The person who has no religious feeling is in a state of spiritual death; she lacks the powerful, life-giving influence of the Spirit of God upon her heart." Our relationship with God is more than an emotional experience, but we should be able to love God in the emotive sense. We cannot dismiss emotion altogether or we find ourselves relating to God with our minds but not our hearts.

At the other extreme are those who gravitate toward reason without emotion. Some people seem more devoted to an intellectual knowledge of God and God's Word than they are to a meaningful relationship with Christ, the Living Word. Again, Jonathan Edwards addresses the need for balance: "We don't want to be merely emotionally excited, without any real transformation of our souls—but neither do we want our faith to be merely a dry, intellectual exercise."

It's possible to study and probe the Bible so thoroughly that we have dissected it until it's dead (so to speak). That is to say that we no longer feel anything toward the Living Word because we have reduced the Bible to propositional truths to be defended. Some people get so caught up in theology that they miss out on the emotional aspects of a dynamic relationship. Instead, their emotions might be focused on presenting a passionate defense for their view of eschatology, the study of end times, so that becomes all that they study or talk about. Or maybe their passion is for apologetics, a defense of the faith, and they spend all their energy trying to rationally argue other people into the kingdom of God. While these are valuable areas of study, we must not neglect the greater value of having a loving relationship with Jesus, the Living Word.

We are most healthy when we allow our intellect to balance our emotions and allow our emotions to enliven our intellect. Inspiration is emotion influenced by reason or, conversely, reason infused with emotion. Inspiration involves arousing the intellect and emotions to motivate action. To say that something inspired me does not mean that it made me feel good but that it moved me emotionally in such a way that I made an intellectual decision to change or take action. For example, perhaps news of an earthquake inspired you to donate blood. You were moved by compassion and wanted to do something to help.

Jonathan Edwards also addresses the need for our love to motivate our actions: "Religion is mostly love, but true religion is not merely warm feelings; it must be expressed by practical active love. In the same way, friendship between earthly friends is mostly love, but it is the sort of love that carries them through fire and water for each other." Love isn't just feeling something or thinking something, it's doing something. We respond to God's love for us by loving Him with our lives—and that involves action.

An Audience of One

Now, let's get back to David. When David brought the ark of the covenant to Jerusalem, he was filled with so much emotion that "David was dancing before the Lord with all his might, and... Michal the daughter of Saul looked out of the

87

window and saw King David leaping and dancing before the Lord; and she despised him in her heart" (2 Samuel 6:14, 16). David's wife was embarrassed by his exuberant exhibition, but David was celebrating a special occasion. He didn't care what others thought.

The Bible doesn't indicate whether David was a good dancer or not. Baseball games I've attended often feature "bad dancing" between innings, where music is played in the stadium, and cameras scan the crowd for the worst dancers to display on the big screen. Some people really are bad dancers, so it's possible that David danced through the city like a chicken. Maybe he made a fool of himself because dancing wasn't his gifting, but he danced anyway as a spontaneous response of joy at the Lord's presence entering Jerusalem.

David's wife, Michal, with a less emotional personality, didn't like his public display of emotion. When David returned home, she told him that he had made a fool of himself by removing his royal robes and adornments and dancing in the street with the common folks. So it wasn't his bad dancing that she despised, but his behavior that she thought was inappropriate for a king. Michal was the daughter of King Saul, so she may have thought, "My father would never have done that."

We need to beware of the judgmental attitude of Michal in our own lives. We all have our own preference about how we relate to God, but we must be careful not to judge others according to our personal preferences or even according to our talents. Not everyone sings like a nightingale. I sing like a crow, but God doesn't mind. I can caw at God all day long, and He loves it because I'm using the gifts that He gave me. Well... maybe it's not a gift, but He gave me this voice, so I must sing just the way He likes it.

David replied to Michal's criticism, saying: "It was before the Lord, who chose me above your father and above all his house, to appoint me ruler over the people of the Lord, over Israel; therefore I will celebrate before the Lord. I will be more lightly esteemed than this and will be humble in my own eyes, but with the maids of whom you have spoken, with them I will be distinguished" (2 Samuel 6:21–22). David knew that he had an audience of One. Only God's attention and approval mattered. David didn't care what other people thought of him. He was willing to make a fool of himself and humble himself before the Lord because he knew that, in God's eyes, he was no fool.

Sometimes we seek the attention and approval of others, but we need to remind ourselves that God's attention and approval are all that matter. We have an audience of One. As we love God with our lives, we develop confidence in our relationship with Him. Eventually, we realize that, no matter what other people think or what may happen, God is enough.

STUDY QUESTIONS

1. How did young David come to have such great confidence in God that he was willing to face Goliath when the adults in the army were scared (1 Samuel 17:37, 47)? What does this tell us about the difference between years with God and experience with God?

2. What is worship? What is the difference between true and false worship (see John 4:23 and Isaiah 29:13)?

3. When David offered a sacrifice to God, what sentiment did he express that indicated he gave to God from the heart and not from ritual obedience (see 1 Chronicles 21:22, 24)?

4. In Psalm 50:15, what does God say about the interactive nature of worship? Explain.

5. When, where, or how do you feel closest to God? Do you relate to God more with your heart or with your mind?

6. When David was dancing before the Lord, what was his wife, Michal, thinking (2 Samuel 6:14, 16)? How can someone who is outwardly expressive be sensitive to others who may not be comfortable with such expressions? Likewise, how can someone who is inwardly expressive be sensitive to others who may feel confined without outward expressions?

SIX

<hr>

For Better or for Worse
Job

*We have come to know and have believed the love
which God has for us. God is love, and the one who abides
in love abides in God, and God abides in him.*
1 JOHN 4:16

Why should we bother being a Christian? Many people think that being a Christian sounds pretty restrictive. To what end do we give up certain behaviors and adopt others?

Some Christians emphasize a prosperity gospel, suggesting that our obedience to God has a direct correlation with God's blessings for health and wealth in our lives. Yet the Bible makes it clear that God "causes his sun to rise on the evil and the good, and sends rain on the righteous and the unrighteous" (Matthew 5:45). In other words, good things will happen to us whether we are good or evil, and bad things will happen to us whether we are good or evil. So what's the point? Why bother? What do we get out of serving God?

The Bible answers these questions in a surprising place: the book of Job. Is there a correlation between serving God and our health and wealth? If not, then do we serve God for nothing? That is a central question posed in the book of Job. Let's take a closer look to see if we can discover some answers, because there are some concepts here that are essential to developing our faith as we become best friends with God.

Job's Faithful Love

It had been a long day already, for Job had risen before dawn to offer burnt offerings to God. During each day of the seven-day feast, Job's seven sons and three daughters celebrated together at one of their brother's homes. Job had raised his children to love and fear God, but just in case one of them had sinned, Job offered burnt offerings on their behalf.

Then, after working all day in the hot sun, Job wanted to sit in his chair and take a nap, but a servant interrupted him and said, "Master, the Sabeans attacked us and took all five hundred oxen and all five hundred donkeys and they slew all of your servants with the sword. I am the only survivor."

Job sat up, but before he could speak, another servant burst into the room, out of breath from running. "Master, the fire of God... the fire of God... it fell from heaven and burned up all seven thousand of your sheep. The fire burned up all your servants. I am the only survivor." The servant began heaving giant sobs between gasps for air.

Just then, another servant came rushing in: "Master, forgive me. I must interrupt your business. The Chaldeans raided us and took your three thousand camels. We put up a fight, but the Chaldeans slew all of your servants, and I alone escaped to tell you. Forgive us, Master. We have failed you." The servant bowed to the floor.

Job was on the edge of his chair now, but before he could think of what to say to all of this, another servant entered, tripping over the servant on the floor and landing on his knees. He spoke with trembling, "Master, your sons and daughters... they were feasting at their oldest brother's house today, and a giant wind struck the house and the roof collapsed on them. I alone survived. I dug through the rubble to rescue them, but they are all dead, my lord. Your ten children are dead." The servant began to weep.

Job stood up and tore his robe. He unsheathed the knife at his waistband and shaved his head, dropping handfuls of gray hair on the floor. The four servants watched their master as he fell to the ground and said, "I was born with nothing and I shall die with nothing. The Lord gave and the Lord has taken away. Blessed be the name of the Lord." The servants were amazed that Job did not blame God, but rather worshiped Him in the midst of grief.

In the days that followed, boils began to cover Job's entire body and he sat in ashes, scraping his flesh with a piece of clay pottery, trying to ease his pain. Job's wife finally told him, "Curse God and die!" but Job rebuked her, saying, "Don't be foolish. Shall we accept God's blessings but not accept adversity?"

Three of Job's friends arrived to comfort him, but Job was disfigured beyond recognition and he was in great pain, so they wept and mourned for their friend, but no one said a word for seven days.

Job broke the silence by saying, "I wish I had never been born." Then Job's friends began to discuss his great suffering. They pled with Job to confess his sin so that God would remove this punishment, but Job maintained his innocence.

His friends' words of comfort didn't seem very comforting to Job, but he clung to hope in God alone, saying, "Even if God kills me, I will hope in Him."

As Job's suffering continued, he maintained his faith in God, but he began to confront God directly, challenging God to hear and answer.

One day the Lord appeared to Job in a whirlwind, but instead of answering Job's questions, He challenged Job to answer a few questions himself: "Were you there when I created the earth? Can you control light and darkness, moon and stars, rain and tide, birds and beasts?"

Job answered, "What can I possibly say? I am insignificant. I will say no more."

Then God questioned Job further: "Will you condemn me, declaring me to be unjust, in order to justify yourself? Everything under the heavens is mine. Who has given me anything that I am indebted to repay?"

Job confessed, "You can do all things. I spoke about things that I did not understand, but I retract my angry words and I repent."

Then the Lord rebuked Job's friends for teaching a religion of rewards and punishments, and the Lord told them to offer burnt offerings for themselves so that He would not deal with them according to their own teaching. Afterwards, the Lord restored Job and blessed the last days of his life more than at first.

Do We Serve God for Nothing?

Readers who are familiar with the book of Job noticed that I left out an important part of the story because I told it from Job's point of view. However, the Bible gives us an astonishing glimpse into the spiritual realm with a couple of conversations between God and Satan.

God said to Satan, "Have you considered My servant Job? For there is no one like him on the earth, a blameless and upright man, fearing God and turning away from evil" (Job 1:8). Throughout the book, Job maintained his innocence in the face of accusations from his friends. God shared that assessment.

In response to God, Satan posed the central question of the book: "Does Job fear God for nothing?" (Job 1:9). Satan went on to argue that God had protected Job, blessed his work, and increased his possessions, so of course Job was faithful. Satan argued that Job lived an upright life because there were positive benefits for him, but if God removed those benefits, Job would curse God.

God granted permission, so Satan swiftly destroyed Job's wealth and his family, but "Job did not sin nor did he blame God" (Job 1:22). God essentially told Satan, "See, I told you so." Satan raised the stakes and argued that a man will do anything to save his own skin, even curse God. So God granted permission for Satan to destroy Job's health.

Most of the book of Job consists of a dialogue between Job and his friends (chapters 3–37). None of these men had the insight, as we do, about the conversation between God and Satan. They could not have known that Satan had asked if Job feared God for nothing, and yet they had a vigorous discussion of that very question. Job's friends thought that by serving God, good would come to them. They concluded that if good deeds produce good results and bad deeds produce bad results, Job must be suffering the consequences of his unrighteousness. Therefore, they urged Job to confess his sin and repent so that God would restore his life.

Despite being wrongly accused by his friends, Job maintained his innocence and battled not only his pain but their shallow theology. He pointed out that God does not always give people what they deserve, because the wicked live and become powerful and prosperous (Job 21:7, 10–13). The wicked dare to tell God, "Depart from us! We do not even desire the knowledge of Your ways. Who is the Almighty, that we should serve Him, and what would we gain if we entreat Him?" (21:14–15). Again, their discussion came back to the question, "Why should we serve God?"

The question lingers throughout the book of Job, but God gets the last word. Finally, God arrives in a whirlwind and sets the record straight—or does He? At first it seems as if God is answering a different question entirely. God never gives an explanation for Job's suffering. He describes His power in creation, asking Job if he is able to do any of the things that God has done, and says that the Creator doesn't need to explain anything to a creature (Job 38–39). Then, God describes a sea monster that would make Moby Dick tremble: Leviathan. "Can you fill his skin with harpoons, or his head with fishing spears?" asks God rhetorically (Job 41:7). "No one is so fierce that he dares to arouse him; who then is he that can stand before Me?" (41:10).

God's answer seems puzzling to modern readers, but, in ancient mythology, Leviathan was the personification of chaos and evil. For God to say that He controlled Leviathan meant that He could control supernatural powers.

So in the first part of God's answer, He said that He controls the natural powers of all created things (Job 38–39), and in the second part of God's answer He said that He controls the supernatural powers of the world (Job 40–41). Job seems satisfied and replies, "I know that You can do all things, and that no purpose of Yours can be thwarted" (Job 42:2).

How does this answer our question of why we should serve God? Job already understood that we don't serve God for health and wealth, for there is not a direct correlation between behavior and consequence. However, through God's revelation, Job learned that the benefit of serving God is having a relationship with the Creator of the universe, who can control both natural and supernatural powers. That's a mighty powerful friend to have.

God Is Enough

With his friends being little help, Job had no one to turn to except God. However, when God is all you have, you realize that God is all you really need. That's the beautiful truth of the book of Job. If we can accept that God is all we need, it will transform our relationship with God and our perspective on life.

If you lost everything, would God be enough? Suffering reveals the kind of foundation we have built our lives upon. Jesus told a parable about a wise man who built his house on a rock, and when the floods came, the house did not fall because it had a firm foundation. By contrast, a foolish man built his house on the sand, and when the floods came, the house fell (Matthew 7:24–27). If everything we owned and even our families were destroyed, as with Job, would we fall apart? If we do, it serves to demonstrate that up to that point in our lives we have failed to build our lives on a firm foundation. This means that we need to work on the foundation *before* the crisis comes. One way to prepare is to ask ourselves these kinds of questions: *What if I lost everything? Is there anything that I could not bear to lose? What if I lost my family? What if I were sick for the rest of my life?*

I grew up in the Seattle area, so I experienced the eruption of Mount St. Helens firsthand. I was eleven years old at the time, so it was my first real exposure to understanding loss. The evacuation orders forced people to make choices about whether to leave their homes or not, knowing that the decision to stay could result in death. Those who chose to leave packed whatever belongings they could fit in their cars. This made an impression on me, but I was too young to fully appreciate the implications because I didn't have possessions of my own yet.

Later, as a young adult beginning to accumulate possessions, I watched similar news unfold as people were being forced out of their homes by wildfires. In many cases, they had only a few minutes to leave. I recall a reporter asking people what they chose to take with them: photos, treasured heirlooms, and important documents. I put myself in that scenario and asked myself what I would take. I looked at each of my possessions and thought, *Hmm... that could be replaced.* Every year since then I have asked myself the same question. This annual exercise during fire season has shaped my thinking about my possessions. I hold them very loosely. They are merely tools to make life functional. If they were destroyed, I could replace them. To be honest, if I could, I would salvage my computer because it contains my writing, but even if it was destroyed I would have lost what I had written, not my ability to write.

In *What Makes Life Worth Living,* Phillip Keller writes, "If anyone comes into our home and happens to remark that they could use some article in our place, very often I pick it up and give it to them... Not only is the recipient pleased with the new possession, but I am glad to be of some help. The side benefit is that very, very few things accumulate around me." Now that's holding your possessions loosely. Keller also limits his book collection to three hundred books (and writers tend to accumulate lots of books). These are the kinds of disciplines that keep things in proper perspective and help build the foundation for our lives.

What's your foundation made of? If you lost everything, would God be enough?

True Value

Job didn't know if his suffering would ever end, and neither did I during a time of sickness in my life. For six months, the doctors didn't know what was wrong with me. All my blood tests came back normal, except that the level of infection in my blood was too high. My vital organs were fine, so the infection was hiding elsewhere. My temperature would flare up to 102–104 degrees for several days at a time. Antibiotics and even steroids had little or no effect.

During that time I was mostly bed-ridden, and, with no medical answers in sight, it occurred to me that I may have to live like this for the rest of my life. *But,* I wondered, *if I cannot do anything that others perceive as valuable, and if I become a liability to others rather than an asset, what is my value? If I am confined to bed for the rest of my life, how would I define my value and purpose? Would life even be worth living?*

We tend to evaluate ourselves based on how others perceive us, or we measure ourselves by our accomplishments, but our true value comes from the worth God places on us.

Everyone wants to feel loved and appreciated, and everyone wants to feel like he or she has something to contribute to life. We take satisfaction from our work and daily tasks because we perceive them as necessary, important, and perhaps something we are uniquely qualified to do. We even identify ourselves in terms of what we do: a teacher, an engineer, or an insurance agent. We work to achieve power, prestige, or possessions, but it can seem pointless. That's why so many people have a mid-life crisis. Our identity is so misunderstood that when all the things we do are stripped away, we wonder who we are.

God loves us for who we are, not for what we do. Our value to God is found in the unique relationship He can enjoy with each one of us because our personality makes us relate to God like no one else. God delights in us for being spontaneous, fun-loving, serious, sentimental, compassionate, intellectual, or whatever makes us who we are. God made us different so that He could enjoy a relationship with us unlike any other.

Only God can provide a true measure of our worth. Even confined to bed, not contributing to society, I have worth to God. Loving God is the Greatest Commandment because that is all God expects of us. Loving God is also the simplest commandment because if we can do nothing else, we can love the Lord. Did you get that? If I can do nothing else, I can love the Lord, and I can do that from bed. If I love the Lord and cling to Him in my darkest hours, I am a success to God.

As for my illness, it turned out to be a severe sinus infection caused by rare bacteria that don't respond to typical antibiotics. During the six months of my illness, I learned to spend my time letting God love me and loving God—from my bed. Those days were more productive than words can tell. That experience tested my foundation and brought into focus what really mattered: loving God.

Personal suffering shows us what kind of foundation we have built our lives upon. If it reveals that we have failed to build our lives upon a firm foundation, we have the opportunity to ask God for help. As He meets our needs, we experience His love for us and learn to trust Him more. Strengthening our relationship with God serves to strengthen our foundation for life.

Do we serve God for nothing? Of course not. We have the privilege of being best friends with the Creator of the universe, and He controls both natural and supernatural powers. Our relationship with the almighty God sustains us through those "for better or for worse" times, and our confidence in God's love for us grows into an unbreakable bond that holds us together when life falls apart. When we know that loving God is what matters most, we realize that life is worth living, regardless of our circumstances.

Choosing to Walk by Faith

Job walked with God during the best of times and the worst of times. His faith in God was strong enough to sustain him through the dark times. But walking by faith isn't just for superheroes of the Bible, nor is it just for the dark times of our lives. Living by faith is important to becoming best friends with God. How important? The Bible says that "without faith it is impossible to please Him, for he who comes to God must believe that He is and that He is a rewarder of those who seek Him" (Hebrews 11:6). If we want to please God, we must have faith to follow God's lead.

So how do we walk with God? At the most basic level, walking involves two steps. If you are able to move one foot forward, then shift your weight so you can move the other foot forward, you can walk. Walking is simply a matter of repeating those two steps. Our walk with God involves two steps: faith and obedience. We can follow God for the rest of our lives by repeating those two steps.

The Bible defines faith as "the assurance of things hoped for, the conviction of things not seen" (Hebrews 11:1). The Bible also explains that "we walk by faith, not by sight" (2 Corinthians 5:7). People refer to "blind faith" because when we cannot see where we are going, we simply trust God to lead us one step at a time. Taking a step of faith is an act of obedience.

In September 1998, I was working as a retail merchandiser in Seattle when I mentioned to my boss that I was thinking about going to school in Portland, Oregon, the next fall. She was the regional manager for the company, and, to my surprise, she said that one of her employees in Portland had just ended up on disability leave and would be out until January. My boss said that I could fill the position, but I would have to move immediately and I would be out of a job at the first of the year. Suddenly things were happening faster than I planned, but I packed and moved to Portland on faith that God was opening the door for me to attend seminary. Once I arrived in Portland, I put in my application with the school and waited for a reply. To my delight, the school processed my application quickly and I was able to start school in January, just when my job ended. Everything worked out perfectly, so I knew that God's leading had brought me there. I was exactly where God wanted me to be.

When you trust God to lead you—even when you don't know how things will turn out—exciting things happen. We don't have to figure out all the pieces of life in advance. God will give us just enough information when we need it. Walking with God requires two steps: faith and obedience.

We learn to trust God one step at a time. Each step may be a step of faith on a path we can't see, but when we reach certain points along the way, we can look back and see the wisdom of God's leading. A year later, during Christmas break at seminary, I had grown increasingly uncomfortable with registering for a full course load for spring semester. Perhaps I felt uncertain about which degree to pursue, or perhaps I was reluctant to accumulate more student loans. Whatever the underlying cause, I decided to register for only four credits. At the time, I had no way of knowing God's wisdom behind this decision.

Two mornings later, I woke up with one dilated eye. This led to a diagnosis of a neurological disease. My eye would be permanently dilated. If you've ever had an eye exam in which the doctor dilated your eyes, then you'll know how painfully sensitive to light a dilated eye can be. I was in a great deal of pain, not only from the piercing pain in my eye, but also in the one-inch portion of my brain that controls vision. With one eye dilated and one eye normal, the constant blurred vision made me feel nauseated. It was difficult to drive because I lost my depth perception, and it was almost impossible to drive after dark. Plus, reading was a challenge because the letters were blurred and one side of the page was washed out, like an overexposed photograph. I was glad that God had prompted me to reduce my course load.

I was not angry at God, wondering, "Why me?" However, I was a little scared about my future. I was afraid to find work. It seemed there were so many things I couldn't do, given my physical limitations, that I would be a liability to an employer rather than an asset. Besides, it was difficult to be positive and upbeat enough to find a job when I was uncertain about my abilities. I kept thinking, *If only I had more self-confidence.*

God didn't want to build my self-confidence; He wanted to build my confidence in Him. I had learned to trust God with the big stuff in life, like moving to attend seminary on faith, so I had confidence that God was still in control of my life. However, He was about to teach me that He was in control of the little stuff in life, too.

Life became complicated for awhile. The doctor had prescribed eye drops to force my dilated eye to constrict so that my vision was less blurred and painful. I had to dilute the prescription with regular eye drops at a ratio of 4:1 in an eye-dropper. Then I had to be careful to squeeze only one drop of the diluted solution into my eye. If I didn't get the ratio right or if I got too much in my eye, my pupil would constrict down to a pinhole and I would be nearly blind for a couple of hours. That made me even more nauseated, and all I could do was lie down and close my eyes until the medication wore off. Life seemed so unpredictable from one moment to the next.

I quickly realized that I couldn't control what happened to my body from one minute to the next—but God could. I couldn't control my pupil dilation, blurred vision, headaches, and everything that went along with them. It was during those frustrating months that God taught me to depend on His grace on a moment-by-moment basis. For the first time in my life, I found myself talking to God all day, every day, because I was constantly aware of my need for His help. And guess what? God met my needs. My love and trust for God grew as a result. It's not that I didn't trust Him before. After all, I had experience with His provision in helping me move and many other faith-building incidents. But this forced me to rely on God for the small stuff in life, not just the life-changing decisions.

After five months, God did some amazing things. My brain grew tired of the constant pain, so it blocked the pain receptors so I no longer felt the piercing pain in my eye or in the vision center of my brain. My brain also started receiving vision primarily from the good eye so that my vision was less blurred.

The doctor had warned me that I had a 20-percent chance that the other eye would become dilated, in which case I would be mostly blind. Sure enough, four years later, I woke up one morning with the other eye dilated. It wasn't as bad as I had feared. In fact, I no longer had to use eye drops because now both pupils were the same size—big.

I'm glad that God allowed this neurological disease in my life because it forced me to rely on Him in a new way. However, you don't have to experience something so drastic in order to learn to rely on God. Just start trusting God with one thing at a time, no matter how big or small, and see what God can do. As you learn to walk in faith and obedience, you don't have to make a leap of faith. Baby steps will do fine.

A statement that is often repeated in the pages of the Bible is "the righteous will live by his faith" (Habakkuk 2:4). Living by faith is walking with God one step at a time. When I know that God loves me, I will follow Him because I trust the direction He will lead me, even if I don't know the exact destination. This is the essence of faith in God.

STUDY QUESTIONS

1. How would you respond to someone who said, "Why should I bother becoming a Christian? Right now I can do whatever I want, but if I became a Christian I'd have to give up certain behaviors and adopt others. What would I get out of becoming a Christian?"

2. What insight can we glean from the parable of the wise and foolish builders (see Matthew 7:24–27)? Reflect on the difficult times in your life. What have they revealed about the quality of your foundation? What can you do to make sure your foundation is strong before the storms of life hit?

3. Job learned that the benefit of serving God is having a relationship with the Creator of the universe, who controls both natural powers (Job 38–39) and supernatural powers (Job 40–41). What was Job's response to God in

Job 42:2? How does this make you feel about being best friends with God?

4. If we can accept that God is all we need, it will transform our relationship with Him and our perspective on life. If you lost everything—your career, your income, your possessions, your home, your family, your friends, your health, and maybe even your reputation—would God be enough? Discuss how you would feel or react if you lost some of the things listed above. Which would be most difficult to lose?

5. What do these verses say about living by faith?

    Habakkuk 2:4

    2 Corinthians 5:7

    Hebrews 11:1

    Hebrews 11:6

6. Is it easier for you to trust God for the big stuff in life or for the little daily stuff? Why? What can you do differently? List a specific area of your life in which you can begin to walk in faith and obedience.

SEVEN

Best Friends Forever

Peter

Love covers a multitude of sins.
1 PETER 4:8

Sometimes we sin, so we confess our sin. And then we sin again, so we confess our sin. And then we do it again, so we wonder if God will still forgive us. We wonder if our habitual sins disqualify us from being a Christian and having a relationship with God. We beat ourselves up for our lack of discipline and bolster our determination to do better.

Meanwhile, the question on God's mind is, "Do you love me?"

Sometimes we do great things for God, so we are certain we are on the path to victorious Christian living, and then we blunder. We try to live for God, but, despite our best efforts, we fail. Maybe we didn't just fail privately; maybe we failed in a publicly humiliating way that makes us feel ashamed to face those who know we failed. Although we had hopes of becoming a spiritual leader, we wonder if God can use us at all.

Meanwhile, the question on God's mind is, "Do you love me?"

That's where the apostle Peter found himself one night. Jesus had seen Peter's capabilities and knew his leadership potential. Jesus had even told Peter that he would help establish the early church. Filled with confidence in his relationship with Jesus, Peter told Him that he wouldn't disappoint Him, his best friend. And then he did. Peter denied that he even knew Jesus.

Meanwhile, the question on Jesus' mind was, "Do you love me?"

Peter definitely had ups and downs in his relationship with Jesus, for he tended to be impulsive, brash, and outspoken. Although we can only speculate about what Peter thought and felt on the night that he denied Christ, the biblical account gives us a good basis for considering Peter's spiritual successes and failures. So let's take a closer look at Peter's experiences so we can learn what our own successes and failures mean in our relationship with Jesus, our best friend.

Peter's Dark Night

Peter didn't feel like Jesus' best friend any more. How could he be? A few hours ago Peter had boasted of how he would defend Christ to the end, but now he had denied that he even knew Christ. Three times. When the rooster crowed, Jesus looked right at him. It wasn't a look of "I told you so," and it wasn't a look of "How dare you?" Jesus looked at him with pity. Jesus, in the midst of being on trial, felt pity for Peter. That made it worse.

Peter ran from the courtyard. He ran as hard as he could, but his wailing made it difficult. Tears blinded Peter's eyes and he stumbled on the stairs, so he knelt there weeping in bitter remorse. He was a liar and he knew it. There was no excuse. He wouldn't try to soften it by calling it something else. He had betrayed his best friend. Where he had been confident of being Christ's best friend before, now he was filled with doubt, guilt, and self-loathing. Peter felt lonely, for he had just severed the one relationship that meant everything to him.

A passer-by stepped over Peter on the stairs, so Peter stirred from his grief and looked around. He found a hiding place, a recessed area beneath the stairs. Peter hid himself in the dark crevasse while bittersweet memories flooded over him.

It was more than three years ago that he first met Jesus. Simon, as he was called at that time, had spent the night fishing on the Lake of Gennesaret with his partners, James and John. For some reason the fish eluded them. That morning they were cleaning their nets, anxious to go home for a few hours of sleep. Along came a rabbi, with a crowd of people listening to His teachings. The man climbed into Simon's boat and asked him to put out a little way from the land. The rabbi sat in the boat teaching the Word of God to eager listeners. Although Simon often fell asleep during synagogue after being up all night fishing, he found himself captivated by this man's words. When the rabbi had finished, He told Simon to take the boat out to deep water and put down the nets for a catch.

Simon protested, "We're tired because we worked all night and caught nothing," but there was something in this man's gaze that made it difficult to say no, so Simon added, "but I will do as you say." The nets immediately filled with so many fish that the ropes began to break. Their partners put out in a second boat to help them, but the load was so great that both boats began to sink.

Peter stared at the rabbi in their boat and fell at His feet, pleading, "Go away from me Lord, for I am a sinner."

Peter stirred from his thoughts and pulled his cloak around him, for the night air grew cold. *Some things never change*, he thought. *I was a sinner then. I'm a sinner still. I thought that being around Jesus for all those years had changed me. Apparently not.*

He could pinpoint the day on which he knew he was a changed man. Jesus began asking His disciples, "Who do people say that I am?" They cited various answers and then Jesus asked them, "But who do you say that I am?"

Simon spoke up, "You are the Christ, the Son of the living God."

Jesus looked into his eyes and said, "Bless you, Simon. You did not discover this on your own, but my Father who is in heaven revealed it to you. From this day forth, you are now *Peter*, which means 'rock,' for upon this rock I will build my church, and the gates of hell will not overpower it."

In their culture, to be given a new name signaled a change in identity. After Peter's confession that Jesus was the Christ, the awaited Messiah promised by God in the Scriptures, Jesus gave him a new identity and commissioned Peter to be a leader on Christ's behalf. Peter never felt the same after that, and he always looked back to that day as the day he changed.

Moments of glory were always short-lived for Peter, for after he confessed his belief that Jesus was the Christ, Jesus warned him and the others not to tell anyone. Jesus explained that He would have to suffer and die, but Peter spoke up: "God forbid it. That will never happen to you, the Christ."

Everyone was alarmed when Jesus turned His back to Peter and said, "Get behind Me, Satan! You are a stumbling block to me. You are setting your mind on man's interests, not God's."

Peter pressed himself further into the recessed area beneath the stairs and tucked his bare feet beneath the hem of his cloak. *How could he be a changed man one minute and an instrument of Satan the next?* Peter wondered. *How could he declare that he would die with Jesus and hours later deny that he even knew Jesus?* Perhaps Peter wasn't the changed man that he thought he was. As Peter wrestled with his thoughts, he recalled another one of those moments of glory . . . and shame.

Jesus put the disciples in a boat and told them to cross the lake while He went off to pray. Even with several experienced fishermen among them, the disciples fought the oars all night, for the wind was against them. Then, what they thought was a ghost came walking across the water toward their boat. The disciples were terrified, as if a grim reaper was about to take them to the depths of the sea. Just then, Jesus called out to them, "Don't be afraid. It's just me."

To this day, Peter didn't know what possessed him to do it, but he called out, "Lord, if it is you, command me to come to you on the water."

Jesus said, "Come."

Peter jumped overboard and landed on the surface of the water and began walking toward Jesus. Then, like a baby learning to walk, Peter began to wobble and sink, and he cried, "Lord, save me!" Jesus reached His arms out and caught Peter, then said, "You of little faith, why did you doubt?" Together they walked back to the boat, and the disciples worshiped Jesus, knowing that He was the Son of God.

Moments of glory. Moments of shame. Peter wasn't sure what to make of it. He peeked out from his self-imposed solitary confinement to check the sky. A hint of daylight brightened the horizon. He wondered what would happen to Jesus.

Three days later, Peter's grief and shame lingered over his life like the dense fog on the Sea of Galilee. He was reunited with the other disciples, except for Judas, who had hung himself for betraying Jesus to the authorities. They consoled each other, for each disciple felt as if he had failed his best friend in His hour of need. Peter seemed to move in slow motion until he heard the women report that the tomb was empty. Then Peter ran. It felt good to run. The blood pulsing through his veins made him feel alive again for the first time since he had run from the courtyard in shame. When Peter got to the tomb, he found it just as the women had said.

The disciples hid. They locked themselves in a room together for fear that the Jews would accuse them of stealing the body and come to arrest them. Suddenly, Jesus appeared in their midst. He spoke words of assurance to them, but the only thing that Peter heard was when Jesus looked him in the eyes and said to them all, "If you forgive the sins of any, their sins have been forgiven them." Peter looked away, still filled with shame.

After many days, when they felt the danger of arrest was past, the disciples came out of seclusion. Peter announced, "I'm going fishing." The other disciples went with him. They spent all night in the boat but caught nothing.

At dawn, a man on the shore called out to them, "Did you catch anything?"

"No," they replied.

"Throw the net on the other side of the boat and you will," said the man.

They cast their nets and caught so many fish they couldn't haul them in. John elbowed Peter and pointed to the shore, "It is the Lord." Immediately, Peter jumped overboard and swam to shore. When he got there, Jesus was cooking fish and bread for them.

After the disciples ate breakfast with Jesus, the Lord said to Peter, in front of the others, "Simon, do you love me more than these?"

"Yes, Lord. You know that I love you."

Jesus said, "Tend my lambs."

Peter wondered what that meant. Then Jesus said again, "Simon, do you love me?"

"Yes, Lord, you know that I love you."

"Shepherd my sheep," said Jesus.

Peter glanced around at the other disciples, feeling awkward. Once again, Jesus asked, "Simon, do you love me?"

Peter began to cry. "Lord, you know all things; you know that I love you."

"Tend my sheep."

Tears streamed down Peter's face, but they were no longer tears of shame and remorse; they were healing tears.

Love and Loyalty

Just when we think that we have resolved the question about God's love for us, something will happen in our lives that shakes us to the foundation. It may be something we did, something someone did to us, or something that just happened. Whatever the cause, we find ourselves back where we started, wondering if God still loves us, if He is still our friend.

That's where Peter found himself on the night that he denied Christ. Yet he began the evening with great confidence.

Peter and the other disciples made some bold claims about their loyalty to Jesus. At the Passover meal, Jesus announced that one of them would betray Him. They each denied it: "Surely not I?" This began a debate among them about which one was the greatest as they each boasted of their loyalty (Luke 22:23–24). Then, as if to end the argument, Jesus told them, "You will all fall away." The disciples refused to believe it. Peter said, "Even though all may fall away, yet I will not" (Mark 14:29). Jesus said that before the night was over, Peter would deny Him three times. Peter insisted, "Even if I have to die with You, I will not deny You!" Peter tends to get a bad reputation over his vow of loyalty, but the Bible says "they all were saying the same thing also" (Mark 14:31).

All twelve disciples claimed that they would remain loyal, even if they had to die with Jesus. Judas went off to betray Jesus to the Jewish authorities, and Jesus took the other eleven to the garden of Gethsemane. When Judas arrived with the Jewish officers and the Roman soldiers, it appears as though the eleven remained true to their promise. Most of the gospels report that a large crowd came to arrest Jesus, but John says that Judas brought officers from the chief priests and the Pharisees, and they were accompanied by a Roman cohort (John 18:3). A Roman cohort consisted of a thousand soldiers. Facing a vast number of trained soldiers, this little group of disciples, with only two swords among them, said, "Lord, shall we strike with the sword?" (Luke 22:49).

I would say that's some serious loyalty and courage in the face of impossible odds. The disciples were prepared to fight. Peter drew his sword and struck the slave of the high priest, cutting off his ear (John 18:10). Jesus put a stop to the violence. He healed the poor slave and then submitted himself to the soldiers.

The disciples were ready to fight and die for their master, but He would not let them. Jesus even asked that the disciples be released (John 18:8). At this point, "all the disciples left Him and fled" (Matthew 26:56). This does not sound as if they fled in fear but that they fled in confusion. They did not know how to help Jesus, for He did not resist arrest, and He didn't seem to want their help.

It's amazing what these disciples were willing to do for their best friend, Jesus. This kind of devotion goes beyond merely obeying the commands of their master. This is the stuff heroes and martyrs are made of, and yet the disciples are often characterized as a bunch of cowards who ran for their lives.

Peter and John followed Jesus to the house of the high priest, where Peter waited in the courtyard for the outcome, warming himself by the fire. Peter, who had the courage to draw swords against a Roman cohort, now trembled when a servant girl identified him as a companion of Jesus (John 18:15–18, 23–27). What happened? Peter was alone. He was separated from the one relationship that gave him strength and courage to defy even the laws of nature, as when he walked on water.

Our relationship with God gives us the same kind of strength and courage. Every moment of every day, we choose whether to maintain that relationship or not. Jesus spoke of our dependent relationship when He said: "I am the vine, you are the branches; he who abides in Me and I in him, he bears much fruit, for apart from Me you can do nothing" (John 15:5). Apart from our relationship with Him, we can do nothing.

When we live wholeheartedly with God, we will have the confidence to walk on water, so to speak. When we hold back even a small part of our hearts and lives, we have separated ourselves from our source of strength. That is when we fail.

A Fisherman's Friend

Peter is one of my favorite Bible personalities because I can relate to his tendency to charge ahead into the unknown. When Peter saw a figure walking on the water, he didn't cower in the boat. He said, "If it is you, Jesus, then prove it! Command me to come to you on the water!" I'd have been right there with Peter, wondering why those words came out of my mouth. *What was I thinking?* Then, after the exhilarating experience of walking on water, I would have been undaunted by the fact that I got wet. In fact, I would have shown up the next day in a wetsuit and said, "Okay, Jesus, let's try that again." Never mind the fact that the wetsuit indicates that I know I'll get wet again. Practice makes perfect, right?

Like Peter, I'm also a little too quick to speak. Peter became the spokesperson for the disciples because he wasn't afraid to say the things that everyone else was thinking. Sometimes he would get overly enthusiastic and say things without really thinking things through. Other times he would say things that seemed completely reasonable and Jesus would rebuke him, as when Jesus foretold His death and Peter said, "God forbid it." Jesus responded, "Get behind Me, Satan!" (Matthew 16:21–23). After that rebuke, I would have been afraid to say anything... for at least ten minutes.

Whenever we fail, our inclination might be to wonder if God still loves us after what we've done. And yet, after Peter's denials, Jesus didn't assure him by saying, "I still love you, Peter." Instead, Jesus posed the question, "Do you love me?"

Let's look at the context of what happened. When Jesus announced that He would be betrayed by one of His disciples, they all denied it and began arguing about which one of them was His greatest disciple (Luke 22:23–24). In the midst of all the boasting, Peter had boldly claimed to Jesus: "Even though all may fall away because of You, I will never fall away" and "Even if I have to die with You, I will not deny You" (Matthew 26:33, 35). Peter boasted of being Jesus' greatest disciple, His most loyal follower, and His best friend. So when Jesus asked Peter, "Do you love me more than these?" He was reminding Peter of his bold claims to have more love and loyalty for Christ than the other disciples.

Jesus' question gave Peter the opportunity to acknowledge his sin of pride—a sin that was now all too clear to Peter in light of his failure. Peter answered with humility, "Yes, Lord; you know that I love you." His failure had deflated his pride so he would no longer claim to love Jesus more than the other disciples. He simply admitted that he loved Jesus and left it at that.

Then, by asking Peter to affirm his love three times, Jesus gave Peter the opportunity to acknowledge that he had denied Christ three times. Peter was grieved because Jesus repeated the question three times. It was painful for him to admit that he had failed his best friend, but confession of sin brings forgiveness and healing.

When we fail Jesus, we can experience forgiveness and healing by confessing our sins. The Bible assures us that "If we confess our sins, He is faithful and righteous to forgive us our sins and to cleanse us from all unrighteousness" (1 John 1:9). Confession restores our relationship with our best friend, Jesus.

Remember, if Jesus had not died on the cross Peter would have died in his sins—as would we. The cross of Christ secured our ability to be reconciled with God and enjoy a relationship with Him (Romans 5:8–10). Although sin may interrupt that relationship, it will never sever it. The Bible says that nothing will be able to separate us from the love of God (Romans 8:38–39) and "Therefore there is now no condemnation for those who are in Christ Jesus" (Romans 8:1).

Paul declared that people "should repent and turn to God, performing deeds appropriate to repentance" (Acts 26:20). Repentance isn't just a matter of sheer determination to never commit a particular sin again. We are changed from the inside, out. Therefore, repentance makes inward change an outward reality. I think many times we struggle to overcome a habitual sin because we are trying to change from the outside by modifying our behavior. Genuine, lasting change happens from the inside. In fact, it is a work of God in our lives.

Our best defense against sin is to ask God to change us on the inside so that our life produces good fruit instead of sin. Jesus said, "He who abides in Me and I in him, he bears much fruit" and "My Father is glorified by this, that you bear much fruit, and so prove to be My disciples" (John 15:5, 8). A healthy branch receives the life-giving resources of the vine, and therefore it produces healthy fruit. A branch that is not fully connected to the vine does not receive enough life-sustaining resources, so it will produce small, unhealthy fruit or none at all. In fact, the branch will eventually wither and die without the flow of the vine. So what appears on the outside—the health of the branch and the quality of its fruit—is the result of what is happening inside.

Repentance is not a matter of turning over a new leaf, but of becoming connected to the vine and abiding in Christ, the source of our strength. When we sin, we disconnect ourselves from the vine, but confession restores our connection to the vine. The evidence that we are living in Christ is that our lives bear the fruit of Christlike qualities: "The fruit of the Spirit is love, joy, peace, patience, kindness, goodness, faithfulness, gentleness, self-control" (Galatians 5:22–23). These characteristics are called the fruit of the Spirit because the Holy Spirit produces these qualities in our life as we abide in Christ. Think of it this way: as you spend more time with your Best Friend, you will become more like Him.

Free to Fail

Peter's failure serves as a reminder that failure comes when you least expect it and usually in an area where you are most confident. The Bible warns that pride can cause us to fail: "Pride goes before destruction, and a haughty spirit before stumbling" (Proverbs 16:18). And none of us are immune to failure, which is all the more reason to beware: "Therefore let him who thinks he stands take heed that he does not fall" (1 Corinthians 10:12).

Luke records an extended version of the conversation in which Jesus tells Peter that he will deny Him three times. Jesus said to Peter: "Satan has demanded permission to sift you like wheat; but I have prayed for you, that your faith may not fail; and you, when once you have turned again, strengthen your brothers" (Luke 22:31–32). The idea of Satan putting Peter through some difficult times (sifting) is strikingly similar to the Job incident. Here, Jesus prayed for Peter so that his faith would not fail. Peter would fail by denying Christ, but his faith would sustain him through the difficult incident. In contrast, Judas failed by betraying Christ, but his faith failed and he resorted to suicide (Matthew 27:3–5). Jesus indicated that Peter would be restored and once again demonstrate leadership in strengthening his brothers.

Jesus could have instilled in Peter the courage and fortitude to stand strong rather than deny Christ. He could have prevented Peter from failing, but He didn't. Why?

I believe there are two reasons. First, failure brings us face to face with our own limitations and reveals our need for God. We will go on living life independently, facing life's challenges with our own strength, until we realize that we can't do it on our own. Remember, we let God love us when we admit that we need Him. As we let Him meet our needs, we feel God's love for us, and, at the same time, we demonstrate our love for God by bringing our needs to Him.

Second, failure followed by forgiveness increases our capacity to receive love and extend love to others because forgiveness itself is a gesture of love. One time, Jesus was having dinner with a Pharisee when a woman who was a sinner came and washed Jesus' feet with her tears. She wiped His feet with her hair, kissing them and anointing them with perfume. The Pharisee thought this was scandalous, so Jesus told a parable about two men in debt (Luke 7:36–50). One man owed five hundred thousand dollars and the other owed fifty thousand dollars. Neither man was able to repay his debt, so the lender forgave them both. Jesus then made the point that the one who is forgiven more, loves more, and the one who is forgiven little, loves little.

We think that a flawless record is better than one marred by sins and failures. However, God gives us the freedom to fail. Then, as we receive God's forgiveness, we experience God's love for us. In return, we feel greater love for God. We also become more willing to extend the same love and forgiveness to others who fail.

Follow Me

It's easy to follow God when we think the path will lead us through fields of green covered in blue skies, but that's not always the case. Jesus wants us to follow Him no matter what the future holds. After the conversation to restore Peter, Jesus walked with him along the beach and told him that he would die a martyr's death, saying, "When you grow old, you will stretch out your hands and someone else will gird you, and bring you where you do not wish to go." Then Jesus reminded him, "Follow Me!" (John 21:18–19). When we are best friends with Jesus, we will follow Him anywhere because we know that, even if it is difficult, He will be with us each step along the way.

The words "follow me" must have taken Peter's thoughts back to the beginning. Peter, James, and John were partners in a fishing business when they first encountered Jesus (Luke 5:1–10). Jesus climbed in Peter's boat and used it for a pulpit from which to teach the multitudes. After His message, Jesus told Peter to put the boat out in deep water and let down the nets for a catch. Although they had been out all night and were unsuccessful, Peter obeyed, and the nets became so full that the boats began to sink. Jesus said, "Follow Me, and I will make you fishers of men" (Matthew 4:19). On that day, the men left their boats and followed Jesus for the next three years. They had been through so much together since then. That's what best friends are for, right?

Throughout the gospels, the hallmark phrase of discipleship was Jesus' call: "Come, follow Me." At His invitation, many followed, though some did not (Mark 10:21–22). The cost of discipleship was high, forcing disciples to leave behind everything, but the rewards were greater still. For the invitation to discipleship—for them as it is for us today—is the invitation to be best friends with God. And so we find ourselves on a lifelong journey with Jesus, walking with Him through each day, learning to love Him and let Him love us, trusting Him to lead us when we can't see the way, and clinging to Him in our darkest hours through pain, fear, and even failure. He will be with us. He's our best friend.

What an awesome privilege to be friends with the Creator of the universe. The God who scattered the stars across the sky breathed life into our human bodies so that we could be friends. God directs the grand orchestra of nature in a symphony of sound, with oceans roaring and birds singing, but He still hears our thoughts. He brings forth crescendos of color as pink flowers fade away just when the blue flowers burst forth in all their glory, and yet He promises that His loving care for us will sustain us through all the seasons of life.

Best friends with God. Imagine that.

STUDY QUESTIONS

1. Have you ever failed God? How? If the situation occurred again, what would you do differently?

2. Describe three instances in which Peter had moments of glory followed by moments of shame:

   Matthew 14:22–33

   Matthew 16:13–23

   Matthew 26:31–35, 69–75

3. Why is habitual sin difficult to overcome? What is our best defense against sin? How is abiding in Christ (John 15:5) effective in helping us overcome sin?

4. What do these verses say about pride and failure?

   Proverbs 16:18

   1 Corinthians 10:12

5. Jesus could have prevented Peter from failing, but He didn't. Why? What are two benefits of failure?

6. What does the parable of the two debtors teach us (Luke 7:36–50)?

7. Jesus' invitation to discipleship, "Follow Me," is the invitation to be best friends with God. After reading this book, how has your thinking changed about your lifelong journey with Jesus?